EUROPE
AND
THE FAITH

EUROPE
AND
THE FAITH

By

Hilaire Belloc

"Sine auctoritate nulla vita."
"Without authority there is no life."

TAN BOOKS AND PUBLISHERS, INC.
Rockford, Illinois 61105

TAN BOOKS AND PUBLISHERS, INC.
P.O. Box 424
Rockford, Illinois 61105
1992

"We have reached at last, as the final result of that catastrophe three hundred years ago, a state of society which cannot endure, and a dissolution of standards, a melting of the spiritual framework, such that the body politic fails. Men everywhere feel that an attempt to continue down this endless and ever-darkening road is like the piling up of debt. We go further and further from a settlement. Our various forms of knowledge diverge more and more. Authority, the very principle of life, loses its meaning, and this awful edifice of civilization which we have inherited, and which is still our trust, trembles and threatens to crash down. It is clearly insecure. It may fall in any moment. We who still live may see the ruin. But ruin when it comes is not only a sudden, it is also a final, thing.

"In such a crux there remains the historical truth: that this our European structure, built upon the noble foundations of classical antiquity, was formed through, exists by, is consonant to, and will stand only in the mold of, the Catholic Church.

"Europe will return to the Faith, or she will perish.

"The Faith is Europe. And Europe is the Faith."

—From page 191.

TABLE OF CONTENTS

EUROPE
AND
THE FAITH

INTRODUCTION

THE CATHOLIC CONSCIENCE OF HISTORY

I say the Catholic "conscience" of history—I say "con-science"—that is, an intimate knowledge through identity: the intuition of a thing which is one with the knower—I do not say "The Catholic Aspect of History." This talk of "aspects" is modern and therefore part of a decline: it is false, and therefore ephemeral: I will not stoop to it. I will rather do homage to truth and say that there is no such thing as a Catholic "aspect" of European history. There is a Protestant aspect, a Jewish aspect, a Mohammedan aspect, a Japanese aspect, and so forth. For all of these look on Europe from without. The Catholic sees Europe from within. There is no more a Catholic "aspect" of European history than there is a man's "aspect" of himself.

Sophistry does indeed pretend that there is even a man's "aspect" of himself. In nothing does false philosophy prove itself more false. For a man's way of perceiving himself (when he does so honestly and after a cleansing examination of his mind) is in line with his Creator's, and therefore with reality: he sees from within.

Let me pursue this metaphor. Man has in him conscience, which is the voice of God. Not only does he know by this that the outer world is real, but also that his own personality is real.

When a man, although flattered by the voice of another, yet says within himself, "I am a mean fellow," he has hold of reality. When a man, though maligned of the world, says to himself of himself, "My purpose was just," he has hold of reality. He knows himself, for he is himself. A man does not know an infinite amount about himself. But the finite amount he does

1

know is all in the map; it is all part of what is really there. What he does not know about himself would, did he know it, fit in with what he does know about himself. There are indeed "aspects" of a man for all others except these two, himself and God Who made him. These two, when they regard him, see him as he is; all other minds have their several views of him; and these indeed are "aspects," each of which is false, while all differ. But a man's view of himself is not an "aspect": it is a comprehension.

Now then, so it is with us who are of the Faith and the great story of Europe. A Catholic as he reads that story does not grope at it from without, he understands it from within. He cannot understand it altogether, because he is a finite being; but he is also that which he has to understand. The Faith is Europe, and Europe is the Faith.

The Catholic brings to history (when I say "history" in these pages I mean the history of Christendom) self-knowledge. As a man in the confessional accuses himself of what he knows to be true and what other people cannot judge, so a Catholic, talking of the united European civilization, when he blames it, blames it for motives and for acts which are his own. He himself could have done those things in person. He is not relatively right in his blame, he is absolutely right. As a man can testify to his own motive, so can the Catholic testify to unjust, irrelevant, or ignorant conceptions of the European story; for he knows why and how it proceeded. Others, not Catholic, look upon the story of Europe externally as strangers. *They* have to deal with something which presents itself to them partially and disconnectedly, by its phenomena alone: *he* sees it all from its center in its essence, and together.

I say again, renewing the terms, The Church is Europe: and Europe is The Church.*

---

*Far from denying the universality of the Roman Catholic Church, the author is rather showing that the Church was, by God's will and Providence, "incarnated" in and shaped by European civilization, centered in Rome (see page 19), and that on its human side the Catholic Church is Roman and European.

The Catholic conscience of history is not a conscience which begins with the development of the Church in the basin of the Mediterranean. It goes back much further than that. The Catholic understands the soil in which that plant of the Faith arose. In a way that no other man can, he understands the Roman military effort; why that effort clashed with the gross Asiatic and merchant empire of Carthage; what we derived from the light of Athens; what food we found in the Irish and the British, the Gallic tribes, their dim but awful memories of immortality; what cousinship we claim with the ritual of false but profound religions, and even how ancient Israel (the little violent people, before they got poisoned, while they were yet National in the mountains of Judea) was, in the old dispensation at least, central and (as we Catholics say) sacred: devoted to a peculiar mission.

For the Catholic the whole perspective falls into its proper order. The picture is normal. Nothing is distorted to him. The procession of our great story is easy, natural, and full. It is also final.

But the modern Catholic, especially if he is confined to the use of the English tongue, suffers from a deplorable (and it is to be hoped), a passing accident. No modern book in the English tongue gives him a conspectus of the past; he is compelled to study violently hostile authorities, North German (or English-copying North German), whose knowledge is never that of the true and balanced European.

He comes perpetually across phrases which he sees at once to be absurd, either in their limitations or in the contradictions they connote. But unless he has the leisure for an extended study, he cannot put his finger upon the precise mark of the absurdity. In the books he reads—if they are in the English language at least—he finds things lacking which his instinct for Europe tells him should be there; but he cannot supply their place because the man who wrote those books was himself ignorant of such

---

It is to this Church that Our Lord wills that the entire world be converted. Moreover, Western Civilization (i.e., the Roman and European civilization) was profoundly shaped by the Roman Catholic Church.—*Editor*, 1992.

things, or rather could not conceive them.

I will take two examples to show what I mean. The one is the present battlefield of Europe: a large affair not yet cleared, concerning all nations and concerning them apparently upon matters quite indifferent to the Faith. It is a thing which any stranger might analyze (one would think) and which yet no historian explains.

The second I deliberately choose as an example particular and narrow: an especially doctrinal story. I mean the story of St. Thomas of Canterbury, of which the modern historian makes nothing but an incomprehensible contradiction; but which is to a Catholic a sharp revelation of the half-way house between the Empire and modern nationalities.

As to the first of these two examples: Here is at last the Great War [World War I] in Europe: clearly an issue—things come to a head. How came it? Why these two camps? What was this curious grouping of the West holding out in desperate Alliance against the hordes that Prussia drove to a victory apparently inevitable after the breakdown of the Orthodox Russian shell? Where lay the roots of so singular a contempt for our old order, chivalry and morals, as Berlin then displayed? Who shall explain the position of the Papacy, the question of Ireland, the aloofness of old Spain?

It is all a welter if we try to order it by modern, external— especially by any materialist or even skeptical—analysis. It was not climate against climate—that facile materialist contrast of "environment," which is the crudest and stupidest explanation of human affairs. It was not race—if indeed any races can still be distinguished in European blood save broad and confused appearances, such as Easterner and Westerner, short and tall, dark and fair. It was not—as another foolish academic theory (popular some years ago) would pretend—an economic affair. There was here no revolt of rich against poor, no pressure of undeveloped barbarians against developed lands, no plan of exploitation, nor of men organized, attempting to seize the soil of less fruitful owners.

How came these two opponents into being, the potential

antagonism of which was so strong that millions willingly suffered their utmost for the sake of a decision?

That man who would explain the tremendous judgment on the superficial test of religious differences among modern "sects" must be bewildered indeed! I have seen the attempt made in more than one journal and book, enemy and Allied. The results are lamentable!

Prussia indeed, the protagonist, was atheist. But her subject provinces supported her exultantly, Catholic Cologne and the Rhine and tamely Catholic Bavaria. Her main support—without which she could not have challenged Europe—was that very power whose sole reason for being was Catholicism: the House of Hapsburg-Lorraine which, from Vienna, controlled and consolidated the Catholic against the Orthodox Slav: the House of Hapsburg-Lorraine was the champion of Catholic organization in Eastern Europe.

The Catholic Irish largely stood apart.

Spain, not devout at all, but hating things not Catholic because those things are foreign, was more than apart. Britain had long forgotten the unity of Europe. France, a protagonist, was notoriously divided within herself over the religious principle of that unity. No modern religious analysis such as men draw up who think of religion as opinion will make anything of all this. Then why was there a fight? People who talk of "Democracy" as the issue of the Great War may be neglected: Democracy—one noble, ideal, but rare and perilous, form of human government—was not at stake. No historian can talk thus. The essentially aristocratic policy of England now turned to a plutocracy, the despotism of Russia and Prussia, the immense complex of all other great modern states gives such nonsense the lie.

People who talk of "A struggle for supremacy between the two Teutonic champions Germany and England" are less respectable still. England is not Teutonic, and was not protagonist. The English Cabinet decided by but the smallest possible majority (a majority of one) to enter the war. The Prussian Government never dreamt it would have to meet England at all.

There is no question of so single an issue. The world was at war. Why? No man is an historian who cannot answer from the past. All who can answer from the past, and are historians, see that it is the historical depth of the European faith, not its present surface, which explains all.

The struggle was against Prussia.

Why did Prussia arise? Because the imperfect Byzantine evangelization of the Eastern Slavonic Plains just failed to meet, there in Prussia, the western flood of living tradition welling up from Rome. Prussia was an hiatus. In that small neglected area neither half cultivated from the Byzantine East nor fully from the Roman West rose a strong garden of weeds. And weeds sow themselves. Prussia, that is, this patch of weeds, could not extend until the West weakened through schism. It had to wait till the battle of the Reformation died down. But it waited. And at last, when there was opportunity, it grew prodigiously. The weed patch overran first Poland and the Germanies, then half Europe. When it challenged all civilization at last it was master of a hundred and fifty million souls.

What are the tests of this war? In their vastly different fashions they are Poland and Ireland—the extreme islands of tenacious tradition: the conservators of the Past through a national passion for the Faith.

The Great War was a clash between an uneasy New Thing which desired to live its own distorted life anew and separate from Europe, and the old Christian rock. This New Thing is, in its morals, in the morals spread upon it by Prussia, the effect of that great storm wherein three hundred years ago Europe made shipwreck and was split into two. This war was the largest, yet no more than the recurrent, example of that unceasing wrestle: the outer, the unstable, the untraditional—which is barbarism—pressing blindly upon the inner, the traditional, the strong—which is Ourselves: which is Christendom: which is Europe.

Small wonder that the Cabinet at Westminster hesitated!

We used to say during the war that if Prussia conquered, civilization failed, but that if the Allies conquered, civilization was re-established—What did we mean? We meant, not that the New Barbarians could not handle a machine: They can. But we meant that they had learnt all from us.

We meant that they cannot *continue of themselves*; and that we can. We meant that they have no roots.

When we say that Vienna was the tool of Berlin, that Madrid should be ashamed, what do we mean? It has no meaning save that civilization is one and we its family: That which challenged us, though it controlled so much which should have aided us and was really our own, was external to civilization and did not lose that character by the momentary use of civilized Allies.

When we said that "the Slav" failed us, what did we mean? It was not a statement of race. Poland is Slav, so is Serbia: they were two vastly differing states, and yet both with us. It meant that the Byzantine influence was never sufficient to inform [i.e., form the soul of] a true European state or to teach Russia a national discipline; because the Byzantine Empire, the tutor of Russia, was cut off from us, the Europeans, the Catholics, the heirs, who are the conservators of the world.

The Catholic Conscience of Europe grasped this war—with apologies where it was in the train of Prussia, with affirmation where it was free. It saw what was toward. It weighed, judged, decided upon the future—the two alternative futures which lie before the world.

All other judgments of the war made nonsense: You had, on the Allied side, the most vulgar professional politicians and their rich paymasters shouting for "Democracy"; pedants mumbling about "Race." On the side of Prussia (the negation of nationality) you have the use of some vague national mission of conquest divinely given to the very various Germans and the least competent to govern. You would come at last (if you listened to such varied cries) to see the Great War as a mere folly, a thing without motive, such as the emptiest internationals conceive the thing to have been.

So much for the example of the war. It is explicable as a challenge to the tradition of Europe. It is inexplicable on any other ground. The Catholic alone is in possession of the tradition of

Europe: he alone can see and judge in this matter.

From so recent and universal an example I turn to one local, distant, precise, in which this same Catholic Conscience of European history may be tested.

Consider the particular (and clerical) example of Thomas à Becket: the story of St. Thomas of Canterbury. I defy any man to read the story of Thomas à Becket in Stubbs, or in Green, or in Bright, or in any other of our provincial Protestant handbooks, and to make head or tail of it.

Here is a well-defined and limited subject of study. It concerns only a few years. A great deal is known about it, for there are many contemporary accounts. Its comprehension is of vast interest to history. The Catholic may well ask: "How is it I cannot understand the story as told by these Protestant writers? Why does it not make sense?"

The story is briefly this: A certain prelate, the Primate of England at the time, was asked to admit certain changes in the status of the clergy. The chief of these changes was that men attached to the Church in any way, even by minor orders (not necessarily priests) should, if they committed a crime amenable to temporal jurisdiction, be brought before the ordinary courts of the country instead of left, as they had been for centuries, to their own courts. The claim was, at the time, a novel one. The Primate of England resisted that claim. In connection with his resistance he was subjected to many indignities, many things outrageous to custom were done against him; but the Pope doubted whether his resistance was justified, and he was finally reconciled with the civil authority. On returning to his See at Canterbury he became at once the author of further action and the subject of further outrage, and within a short time he was murdered by his exasperated enemies.

His death raised a vast public outcry. His monarch did penance for it. But *all the points on which he had resisted* were in practice waived by the Church at last. The civil state's original claim was *in practice* recognized at last. Today it appears to be plain justice. The chief of St. Thomas' contentions, for instance, that men in orders should be exempt from the ordinary courts, seems as remote as chain armors.

So far, so good. The opponent of the Faith will say, and has said in a hundred studies—that this resistance was nothing more than that always offered by an old organization to a new development.

Of course it was! It is equally true to say of a man who objects to an aëroplane smashing in the top of his studio that it is the resistance of an old organization to a new development. But such a phrase in no way explains the business; and when the Catholic begins to examine the particular case of St. Thomas, he finds a great many things to wonder at and to think about, upon which his less European opponents are helpless and silent.

I say "helpless" because in their attitude they give up trying to explain. They record these things, but they are bewildered by them. They can explain St. Thomas' particular action simply enough: too simply. He was (they say) a man living in the past. But when they are asked to explain the vast consequences that followed his martyrdom, they have to fall back upon the most inhuman and impossible hypotheses; that "the masses were ignorant"—that is as compared with other periods in human history (what, more ignorant than today?) that "the Papacy engineered an outburst of popular enthusiasm." As though the Papacy were a secret society like modern Freemasonry, with some hidden machinery for "engineering" such things. As though the type of enthusiasm produced by the martyrdom was the wretched mechanical thing produced now by caucus or newspaper "engineering"! As though nothing *besides* such interferences was there to arouse the whole populace of Europe to such a pitch!

As to the miracles which undoubtedly took place at St. Thomas' tomb, the historian who hates or ignores the Faith had (and has) three ways of denying them. The first is to say nothing about them. It is the easiest way of telling a lie. The second is to say that they were the result of a vast conspiracy which the priests directed and the feeble acquiescence of the maim, the halt and the blind supported. The third (and for the moment most popular) is to give them modern journalistic names, sham

Latin and Greek confused, which, it is hoped, will get rid of the miraculous character; notably do such people talk of "auto-suggestion."

Now the Catholic approaching this wonderful story, when he has read all the original documents, understands it easily enough from within.

He sees that the stand made by St. Thomas was not very important in its special claims, and was probably (taken as an isolated action) unreasonable. But he soon gets to see, as he reads and as he notes the rapid and profound transformation of all civilization which was taking place in that generation, that St. Thomas was standing out for a principle, ill clothed in his particular plea, but absolute in its general appreciation: the freedom of the Church. He stood out in particular for what *had* been the concrete symbols of the Church's liberty in the past. The direction of his actions was everything, whether his symbol was well or ill chosen. The particular customs might go. But to challenge the new claims of civil power at that moment was to save the Church. A movement was afoot which might have then everywhere accomplished what was only accomplished in parts of Europe four hundred years later, to wit, a dissolution of the unity and the discipline of Christendom.

St. Thomas had to fight on ground chosen by the enemy; he fought and he resisted in the spirit dictated by the Church. He fought for no dogmatic point, he fought for no point to which the Church of five hundred years earlier or five hundred years later would have attached importance. He fought for things which were purely temporal arrangements; which had indeed until quite recently been the guarantee of the Church's liberty, but which were in his time upon the turn of becoming negligible. *But the spirit in which he fought was a determination that the Church should never be controlled by the civil power,* and the spirit against which he fought was the spirit which either openly or secretly believes the Church to be an institution merely human, and therefore naturally subjected, as an inferior, to the processes of the monarch's (or, worse, the politician's) law.

A Catholic sees, as he reads the story, that St. Thomas was

obviously and necessarily to lose, in the long run, every concrete point on which he had stood out, and yet he saved throughout Europe the ideal thing for which he was standing out. A Catholic perceives clearly why the enthusiasm of the populace rose: the guarantee of the plain man's healthy and moral existence against the threat of the wealthy, and the power of the State—the self-government of the general Church, had been defended by a champion up to the point of death. For the morals enforced by the Church are the guarantee of freedom.

Further the Catholic reader is not content, as is the non-Catholic, with a blind, irrational assertion that the miracles could not take place. He is not wholly possessed of a firm and lasting faith that no marvelous events ever take place. He reads the evidence. He cannot believe that there was a conspiracy of falsehood (in the lack of all proof of such conspiracy): He is moved to a conviction that events so minutely recorded and so amply testified, happened. Here again is the European, the chiefly reasonable man, the Catholic, pitted against the barbarian skeptic with his empty, unproved, mechanical dogmas of material sequence.

And these miracles, for a Catholic reader, are but the extreme points fitting in with the whole scheme. He knows what European civilization was before the twelfth century. He knows what it was to become after the sixteenth. He knows why and how the Church would stand out against a certain itch for change. He appreciates why and how a character like that of St. Thomas would resist. He is in no way perplexed to find that the resistance failed on its technical side. He sees that it succeeded so thoroughly in its spirit as to prevent, in a moment when its occurrence would have been far more dangerous and general than in the sixteenth century, the overturning of the connection between Church and State.

The enthusiasm of the populace he particularly comprehends. He grasps the connection between that enthusiasm and the miracles which attended St. Thomas' intercession; not because the miracles were fantasies, but because a popular recognition of deserved sanctity is the later accompaniment and the recipient of miraculous power.

It is the details of history which require the closest analysis. I have, therefore, chosen a significant detail with which to exemplify my case.

Just as a man who thoroughly understands the character of the English squires and of their position in the English countrysides would have to explain at some length (and with difficulty) to a foreigner how and why the evils of the English large estates were, though evils, national; just as a particular landlord case of peculiar complexity or violent might afford him a special test; so the martyrdom of St. Thomas makes, for the Catholic who is viewing Europe, a very good example whereby he can show how well he understands what is to other men not understandable, and how simple is to him, and how human, a process which, to men not Catholic, can only be explained by the most grotesque assumptions; as that universal contemporary testimony must be ignored; that men are ready to die for things in which they do not believe; that the philosophy of a society does not permeate that society; or that a popular enthusiasm ubiquitous and unchallenged is mechanically produced to the order of some center of government! All these absurdities are connoted in the non-Catholic view of the great quarrel, nor is there any but the Catholic conscience of Europe that explains it.

The Catholic sees that the whole of the à Becket business was like the struggle of a man who is fighting for his liberty and is compelled to maintain it (such being the battleground chosen by his opponents) upon a privilege inherited from the past. The non-Catholic simply cannot understand it and does not pretend to understand it.

Now let us turn from this second example, highly definite and limited, to a third quite different from either of the other two and the widest of all. Let us turn to the general aspect of all European history. We can here make a list of the great lines on which the Catholic can appreciate what other men only puzzle at, and can determine and know those things upon which other men make no more than a guess.

The Catholic Faith spreads over the Roman world, not because the Jews were widely dispersed, but because the intellect of antiquity, and especially the Roman intellect, accepted it in its maturity.

The material decline of the Empire is not correlative with, nor parallel to, the growth of the Catholic Church; it is the counterpart of that growth. You have been told "Christianity (a word, by the way, quite unhistorical) crept into Rome as she declined, and hastened that decline." That is bad history. Rather accept this phrase and retain it: "The Faith is that which Rome accepted in her maturity; nor was the Faith the cause of her decline, but rather the conservator of all that could be conserved."

There was no strengthening of us by the advent of barbaric blood; there was a serious emperilling of civilization in its old age by some small (and mainly servile) infiltration of barbaric blood; if civilization so attacked did not permanently fail through old age we owe that happy rescue to the Catholic Faith.

In the next period—the Dark Ages—the Catholic proceeds to see Europe saved against a universal attack of the Mohammedan, the Hun, the Scandinavian: he notes that the fierceness of the attack was such that anything save something divinely instituted would have broken down. The Mohammedan came within three days' march of Tours, the Mongol was seen from the walls of Tournus on the Sâone: right in France. The Scandinavian savage poured into the mouths of all the rivers of Gaul, and almost overwhelmed the whole island of Britain. There was nothing left of Europe but a central core.

Nevertheless Europe survived. In the refloresence which followed that dark time—in the Middle Ages—the Catholic notes not hypotheses but documents and facts; he sees the Parliaments arising not from some imaginary "Teutonic" root—a figment of the academies—but from the very real and present great monastic orders, in Spain, in Britain, in Gaul—never outside the old limits of Christendom. He sees the Gothic architecture spring high, spontaneous and autochthonic, first in the territory of Paris and thence spread outwards in a ring to the Scotch Highlands and to the Rhine. He sees the new Universities, a product of the soul of Europe, re-awakened—he sees the marvelous new civilization of the Middle Ages rising as a transformation of the old Roman society, a transformation wholly from within, and motivated by the Faith.

The trouble, the religious terror, the madnesses of the fifteenth century, are to him the diseases of one body—Europe—in need of medicine.

The medicine was too long delayed. There comes the disruption of the European body at the Reformation.

It ought to be death; but since the Church is not subject to mortal law it is not death. Of those populations which break away from religion and from civilization none (he perceives) were of the ancient Roman stock—save Britain. The Catholic, reading his history, watches in that struggle *England:* not the effect of the struggle on the fringes of Europe, on Holland, North Germany and the rest. He is anxious to see whether *Britain* will fail the mass of civilization in its ordeal.

He notes the keenness of the fight in England and its long endurance; how all the forces of wealth—especially the old families such as the Howards and the merchants of the City of London—are enlisted upon the treasonable side; how in spite of this a tenacious tradition prevents any sudden transformation of the British polity or its sharp severance from the continuity of Europe. He sees the whole of North England rising, cities in the South standing siege. Ultimately he sees the great nobles and merchants victorious, and the people cut off, apparently forever, from the life by which they had lived, the food upon which they had fed.

Side by side with all this he notes that, next to Britain, one land only that was never Roman land, by an accident inexplicable or miraculous, preserves the Faith, and, as Britain is lost, he sees side by side with that loss the preservation of Ireland.

To the Catholic reader of history (though he has no Catholic history to read) there is no danger of the foolish bias against civilization which has haunted so many contemporary writers, and which has led them to frame fantastic origins for institutions the growth of which are as plain as an historical fact can be. He does not see in the pirate raids which desolated the eastern

and southeastern coasts of England in the sixth century the origin of the English people. He perceives that the success of these
small eastern settlements upon the eastern shores, and the spread
of their language westward over the island dated from their
acceptance of Roman discipline, organization and law, from
which the majority, the Welsh to the West, were cut off. He
sees that the ultimate hegemony of Winchester over Britain all
grew from this early picking up of communications with the
Continent and the cutting off of everything in this island save
the South and East from the common life of Europe. He knows
that Christian parliaments are not dimly and possibly barbaric,
but certainly and plainly monastic in their origin; he is not sur-
prised to learn that they arose first in the Pyrenean valleys during
the struggle against the Mohammedans; he sees how probable
or necessary was such an origin just when the chief effort of
Europe was at work in the *Reconquista.*

In general, the history of Europe and of England develops naturally before the Catholic reader; he is not tempted to that succession of theories, self-contradicting and often put forward for
the sake of novelty, which has confused and warped modern
reconstructions of the past. Above all, he does not commit the
prime historical error of "reading history backwards." He does
not think of the past as a groping towards our own perfection
of today. He has in his own nature the nature of its career: he
feels the fall and the rise: the rhythm of a life which is his own.

The Europeans are of his flesh. He can converse with the first
century or the fifteenth; shrines are not odd to him nor oracles;
and if he is the supplanter, he is also the heir of the gods.

1

WHAT WAS THE ROMAN EMPIRE?

The history of European civilization is the history of a certain political institution which united and expressed Europe, and was governed from Rome. This institution was informed at its very origin by the growing influence of a certain definite and organized religion: this religion it ultimately accepted and, finally, was merged in.

The institution—having accepted the religion, having made of that religion its official expression, and having breathed that religion in through every part until it became the spirit of the whole—was slowly modified, spiritually illumined and physically degraded by age. But it did not die. It was revived by the religion which had become its new soul. It re-arose and still lives.

This institution was first known among men as *Republica;* we call it today "The Roman Empire." The Religion which informed and saved it was then called, still is called, and will always be called "The Catholic Church."

Europe is the Church, and the Church is Europe.

It is immaterial to the historical value of this historical truth whether it be presented to a man who utterly rejects Catholic dogma or to a man who believes everything the Church may teach. A man remote in distance, in time, or in mental state from the thing we are about to examine would perceive the reality of this truth just as clearly as would a man who was steeped in its spirit from within and who formed an intimate part of Christian Europe. The Oriental pagan, the contemporary atheist, some supposed student in some remote future, reading history in some place from which the Catholic Faith shall have utterly departed, and to which the habits and traditions of our civilization will therefore be wholly alien, would each, in proportion to his science, grasp as clearly as it is grasped today by the Catholic student who is of European birth, the truth that Europe and the Catholic Church were and are one thing.* The only people who do *not* grasp it (or do not admit it) are those writers of history whose special, local, and temporary business it is to oppose the Catholic Church, or who have a traditional bias against it.

These men are numerous, they have formed, in the Protestant and other anti-Catholic universities, a whole school of hypothetical and unreal history in which, though the original workers are few, their copyists are innumerable: and that school of unreal history is still dogmatically taught in the anti-Catholic centers of Europe and of the world.

Now our quarrel with this school should be, not that it is anti-Catholic—that concerns another sphere of thought—but that it is unhistorical.

To neglect the truth that the Roman Empire with its institutions and its spirit was the sole origin of European civilization; to forget or to diminish the truth that the Empire accepted in its maturity a certain religion; to conceal the fact that this religion was not a vague mood, but a determinate and highly organized corporation; to present in the first centuries some non-existent "Christianity" in place of the existent Church; to suggest that the Faith was a vague agreement among individual holders of opinions instead of what it historically *was,* the doctrine of a fixed authoritative institution; to fail to identify that institution with the institution still here today and still called the Catholic Church; to exaggerate the insignificant barbaric influences which came from outside the Empire and did nothing to modify its spirit; to pretend that the Empire or its religion have at any time ceased to be—that is, to pretend that there has ever been a solution of continuity between the past and the present of Europe—all these pretensions are parts of one historical falsehood.

In all by which we Europeans differ from the rest of mankind

---

* See footnote on page 2.—*Editor,* 1992.

there is *nothing* which was not originally peculiar to the Roman Empire, or is not demonstrably derived from something peculiar to it.

In material objects the whole of our wheeled traffic, our building materials, brick, glass, mortar, cut-stone, our cooking, our staple food and drink; in forms, the arch, the column, the bridge, the tower, the well, the road, the canal; in expression, the alphabet, the very words of most of our numerous dialects and polite languages, the order of still more, the logical sequence of our thought—all spring from that one source. So with implements: the saw, the hammer, the plane, the chisel, the file, the spade, the plough, the rake, the sickle, the ladder; all these we have from that same origin. Of our institutions it is the same story. The divisions and the sub-divisions of Europe, the parish, the county, the province, the fixed national traditions with their boundaries, the emplacement of the great European cities, the routes of communication between them, the universities, the Parliaments, the Courts of Law, and their jurisprudence, all these derive entirely from the old Roman Empire, our well-spring.

It may here be objected that to connect so closely the worldly foundations of our civilization with the Catholic or universal religion of it, is to limit the latter and to make of it a merely human thing.

The accusation would be historically valueless in any case, for in history we are not concerned with the claims of the supernatural, but with a sequence of proved events in the natural order. But if we leave the province of history and consider that of theology, the argument is equally baseless. Every manifestation of divine influence among men must have its human circumstance of place and time. The Church might have risen under Divine Providence in any spot: it did, as a fact, spring up in the high *Greek* tide of the Levant and carries to this day the noble Hellenic garb. It might have risen at any time: it did, as a fact, rise just at the inception of that united Imperial Roman system which we are about to examine. It might have carried for its ornaments and have had for its sacred language the accoutrements and the speech of any one of the other great civilizations, living or dead: of Assyria, of Egypt, of Persia, of China, of the Indies. As a matter of historical fact, the Church was so circumstanced in its origin and development that its external accoutrement and its language were those of the Mediterranean, that is, of Greece and Rome: of the Empire.

Now those who would falsify history from a conscious or unconscious bias against the Catholic Church will do so in many ways, some of which will always prove contradictory of some others. For truth is one, error disparate and many.

The attack upon the Catholic Church may be compared to the violent, continual, but inchoate attack of barbarians upon some civilized fortress; such an attack will proceed now from this direction, now from that, along any one of the infinite number of directions from which a single point may be approached. Today there is attack from the North, tomorrow an attack from the South. Their directions are flatly contradictory, but the contradiction is explained by the fact that each is directed against a central and fixed opponent.

Thus, some will exaggerate the power of the Roman Empire as a pagan institution; they will pretend that the Catholic Church was something alien to that pagan thing; that the Empire was great and admirable before Catholicism came, weak and despicable upon its acceptation of the Creed. They will represent the Faith as creeping like an Oriental disease into the body of a firm Western society which it did not so much transform as liquefy and dissolve.

Others will take the clean contrary line and make out a despicable Roman Empire to have fallen before the advent of numerous and vigorous barbarians (Germans, of course) possessing all manner of splendid pagan qualities—which usually turn out to be nineteenth century Protestant qualities. These are contrasted against the diseased Catholic body of the Roman Empire which they are pictured as attacking.

Others adopt a simpler manner. They treat the Empire and its institutions as dead after a certain date, and discuss the rise of a new society without considering its Catholic and Imperial origins. Nothing is commoner, for instance (in English schools), than for boys to be taught that the pirate raids and settlements of the fifth century in this Island were the "coming of the English," and the complicated history of Britain is simplified for them into a story of how certain bold seafaring pagans (full of all the virtues we ascribe to ourselves today) first devastated, then occupied, and at last, of their sole genius, developed a land which Roman civilization had proved inadequate to hold.

There is, again, a conscious or unconscious error (conscious or unconscious, pedantic or ignorant, according to the degree of learning in him who propagates it) which treats of the religious life of Europe as though it were something quite apart from the general development of our civilization.

There are innumerable text-books in which a man may read the whole history of his own, a European, country, from, say, the fifth to the sixteenth century, and never hear of the Blessed Sacrament: which is as though a man were to write of England in the nineteenth century without daring to speak of newspapers and limited companies. Warped by such historical enormities, the reader is at a loss to understand the ordinary motives of his ancestors. Not only do the great crises in the history of the Church obviously escape him, but much more do the great crises in civil history escape him.

To set right, then, our general view of history it is necessary to be ready with a sound answer to the prime question of all, which is this: "What was the Roman Empire?"

If you took an immigrant coming fresh into the United States today and let him have a full knowledge of all that had happened since the Civil War: if you gave him of the Civil War itself a partial, confused and very summary account: if of all that went before it, right away back to the first colonists, you were to leave him either wholly ignorant or ludicrously misinformed (and slightly informed at that), what then could he make of the problems in American Society, or how would he be equipped to understand the nation of which he was to be a citizen? To give such a man the elements of civic training you must let him know what the Colonies were, what the War of Independence, and what the main institutions preceding that event and created by it. He would have further to know soundly the struggle between North and South, and the principles underlying that struggle. Lastly, and most important of all, he would have to see all this in a correct perspective.

So it is with us in the larger question of that general civilization which is common to both Americans and Europeans, and which in its vigor has extended garrisons, as it were, into Asia and Africa. We cannot understand it today unless we understand what it developed from. What was the origin from which we sprang? What was the Roman Empire?

The Roman Empire was a united civilization, the prime characteristic of which was the acceptation, absolute and unconditional, of one common mode of life by all those who dwelt within its boundaries. It is an idea very difficult for the modern man to seize, accustomed as he is to a number of sovereign countries more or less sharply differentiated, and each separately colored, as it were, by different customs, a different language, and often a different religion. Thus the modern man sees France, French speaking, with an architecture, manners, laws of its own, etc.; he saw (till yesterday) North Germany under the Prussian hegemony, German speaking, with yet another set of institutions, and so forth. When he thinks, therefore, of any great conflict of opinion, such as the discussion between aristocracy and democracy today, he thinks in terms of different countries. Ireland, for instance, is Democratic, England is Aristocratic—and so forth.

Again, the modern man thinks of a community, however united, as something bounded by, and in contrast with, other communities. When he writes or thinks of France he does not think of France only, but of the points in which France contrasts with England, North Germany, South Germany, Italy, etc.

Now the men living in the Roman Empire regarded civic life in a totally different way. All conceivable antagonisms (and they were violent) were antagonisms *within one State*. No differentiation of State against State was conceivable or was attempted.

From the Euphrates to the Scottish Highlands, from the North Sea to the Sahara and the Middle Nile, all was one State.

The world outside the Roman Empire was, in the eyes of the Imperial citizen, a sort of waste. It was not thickly populated, it had no appreciable arts or sciences, it was *barbaric*. That outside waste of sparse and very inferior tribes was something of a menace upon the frontiers, or, to speak more accurately, something of an irritation. But that menace or irritation was never conceived of as we conceive of the menace of a foreign power. It was merely the trouble of preventing a fringe of imperfect, predatory, and small barbaric communities outside the boundaries from doing harm to a vast, rich, thickly populated, and highly organized State within.

The members of these communities (principally the Dutch, Frisian, Rhenish and other Germanic peoples, but also on the other frontiers, the nomads of the desert, and in the West, islanders and mountaineers, Irish and Caledonian) were all tinged with the great Empire on which they bordered. Its trade permeated them. We find its coins everywhere. Its names for most things became part of their speech. They thought in terms of it. They had a sort of grievance when they were not admitted to it. They perpetually begged for admittance.

They wanted to deal with the Empire, to enjoy its luxury, now and then to raid little portions of its frontier wealth.

They never dreamt of "conquest." On the other hand the Roman administrator was concerned with getting barbarians to settle in an orderly manner on the frontier fields, so that he could exploit their labor, with coaxing them to serve as mercenaries in the Roman armies, or (when there was any local conflict) with defeating them in local battles, taking them prisoners and making them slaves.

I have said that the mere number of these exterior men (German, Caledonian, Irish, Slav, Moorish, Arab, etc.) was small compared with the numbers of civilization, and, I repeat, in the eyes of the citizens of the Empire, their lack of culture made them more insignificant still.

At only one place did the Roman Empire have a common frontier with another civilization, properly so called. It was a very short frontier, not one-twentieth of the total boundaries of the

Empire. It was the Eastern or Persian frontier, guarded by spaces largely desert. And though a true civilization lay beyond, that civilization was never of great extent nor really powerful. This frontier was variously drawn at various times, but corresponded roughly to the Plains of Mesopotamia. The Mediterranean peoples of the Levant, from Antioch to Judea, were always within that frontier. They were Roman. The mountain peoples of Persia were always beyond it. Nowhere else was there any real rivalry or contact with the foreigner, and even this rivalry and contact (though "The Persian War" is the only serious *foreign* or equal war in the eyes of all the rulers from Julius Caesar to the sixth century) counted for little in the general life of Rome.

The point cannot be too much insisted upon, nor too often repeated, so strange is it to our modern modes of thought, and so essentially characteristic of the first centuries of the Christian era and the formative period during which Christian civilization took its shape. *Men lived as citizens of one State which they took for granted and which they even regarded as eternal.* There would be much grumbling against the taxes and here and there revolts against them, but never a suggestion that the taxes should be levied by any other than imperial authority, or imposed in any other than the imperial manner. There was plenty of conflict between armies and individuals as to who should have the advantage of ruling, but never any doubt as to the type of function which the "Emperor" filled, nor as to the type of universally despotic action which he exercised. There were any number of little local liberties and customs which were the pride of the separate places to which they attached, but there was no conception of such local differences being antagonistic to the one life of the one State. That State was, for the men of that time, the World.

The complete unity of this social system was the more striking from the fact that it underlay not only such innumerable local customs and liberties, but an almost equal number of philosophic opinions, of religious practices, and of dialects. There was not even one current official language for the educated thought of the Empire: there were two, Greek and Latin.

And in every department of human life there co-existed this very large liberty of individual and local expression, coupled with a complete, and, as it were, necessary unity, binding the whole vast body together. Emperor might suceed Emperor, in a series of civil wars. Several Emperors might be reigning together. The office of Emperor might even be officially and consciously held in commission among four or more men. But the power of the Emperor was always one power, his office one office, and the system of the Empire one system.

It is not the purpose of these few pages to attempt a full answer to the question of how such a civic state of mind came to be, but the reader must have some *sketch* of its development if he is to grasp its nature.

The old Mediterranean world out of which the Empire grew had consisted (before that Empire was complete—say, from an unknown most distant past to 50 B.C.) in two types of society: there stood in it as rare exceptions *States*, or nations in our modern sense, governed by a central Government, which controlled a large area, and were peopled by the inhabitants of many towns and villages. Of this sort was ancient Egypt. But there were also, surrounding that inland sea, in such great numbers as to form the predominant type of society, a series of *Cities,* some of them commercial ports, most of them controlling a small area from which they drew their agricultural subsistence, but all of them remarkable for this, that their citizens drew their civic life from, felt patriotism for, were the soldiers of, and paid their taxes to, not a nation in our sense but a *municipality.*

These cities and the small surrounding territories which they controlled (which, I repeat, were often no more than local agricultural areas necessary for the sustenance of the town) were essentially the sovereign Powers of the time. Community of language, culture, and religion might, indeed, bind them in associations more or less strict. One could talk of the Phoenician cities, of the Greek cities, and so forth. But the individual City was always the unit. City made war on City. The City decided its own customs, and was the nucleus of religion. The God was the God of the city. A rim of such points encircled the eastern and central Mediterranean wherever it was habitable by man. Even the little oasis of the Cyrenaean land with sand on every side, but habitable, developed its city formations. Even on the western coasts of the inland ocean, which received their culture by sea from the East, such City States, though more rare, dotted the littoral of Algeria, Provence and Spain.

Three hundred years before Our Lord was born this moral equilibrium was disturbed by the huge and successful adventure of the Macedonian Alexander.

The Greek City States had just been swept under the hegemony of Macedon, when, in the shape of small but invincible armies, the common Greek culture under Alexander overwhelmed the East. Egypt, the Levant littoral and much more, were turned into one Hellenized (that is, "Greecified") civilization. The separate cities, of course, survived, and after Alexander's death unity of control was lost in various and fluctuating dynasties derived from the arrangements and quarrels of his generals. But the old moral equilibrium was gone and the conception of a general civilization had appeared. Henceforward the Syrian, the Jew, the Egyptian saw with Greek eyes and the Greek tongue was the medium of all the East for a thousand years. Hence are the very earliest names of Christian things, Bishop, Church, Priest, Baptism, Christ, Greek names. Hence all our original documents and prayers are Greek and shine with a Greek light: nor are any so essentially Greek in idea as the four Catholic Gospels.

Meanwhile in Italy one city, by a series of accidents very difficult to follow (since we have only later accounts—and they are drawn from the city's point of view only), became the chief of the City States in the Peninsula. Some few it had conquered in war and had subjected to taxation and to the acceptation of its own laws; many it protected by a sort of superior alliance; with many more its position was ill defined and perhaps in origin had been a position of allied equality. But at any rate, a little after the Alexandrian Hellenization of the East this city had in a slower and less universal way begun to break down the moral equilibrium of the City States in Italy, and had produced between the Apennines and the sea (and in some places beyond the Apen-

nines) a society in which the City State, though of course surviving, was no longer isolated or sovereign, but formed part of a
larger and already definite scheme. The city which had arrived
at such a position, and which was now the manifest capital of
the Italian scheme, was ROME.

Contemporary with the last successes of this development in
Italy went a rival development very different in its nature, but
bound to come into conflict with the Roman because it also was
extending. This was the commercial development of Carthage.
Carthage, a Phoenician, that is, a Levantine and Semitic, colony,
had its city life like all the rest. It had shown neither the aptitude
nor the desire that Rome had shown for conquest, for alliances,
and in general for a spread of its spirit and for the domination
of its laws and modes of thought. The business of Carthage was
to enrich itself: not indirectly as do soldiers (who achieve riches
as but one consequence of the pursuit of arms), but directly,
as do merchants, by using men indirectly, by commerce, and
by the exploitation of contracts.

The Carthaginian occupied mining centers in Spain, and har-
bors wherever he could find them, especially in the Western
Mediterranean. He employed mercenary troops. He made no
attempt to radiate outward slowly step by step, as does the military type, but true to the type of every commercial empire, from
his own time to our own, the Carthaginian built up a scattered
hotchpotch of dominion, bound together by what is today called
the "Command of the Sea."

That command was long absolute and Carthaginian power
depended on it wholly. But such a power could not co-exist with
the growing strength of martial Italy. Rome challenged Carthage;
and after a prodigious struggle, which lasted to within two hundred years of the birth of Our Lord, ruined the Carthaginian
power. Fifty years later the town itself was destroyed by the
Romans, and its territory turned into a Roman province. So
perished for many hundred years the dangerous illusion that the
merchant can master the soldier. But never had that illusion
seemed nearer to the truth than at certain moments in the duel
between Carthage and Rome.

The main consequence of this success was that, by the nature of the struggle, the Western Mediterranean, with all its City States, with its half-civilized Iberian peoples, lying on the plateau of Spain behind the cities of the littoral, the corresponding belt of Southern France, and the cultivated land of Northern Africa, fell into the Roman system, and became, but in a more united way, what Italy had already long before become. The Roman power, or, if the term be preferred, the Roman confederation, with its ideas of law and government, was supreme in the Western Mediterranean and was compelled by its geographical position to extend itself inland further and further into Spain, and even (what was to be of prodigious consequence to the world) into GAUL.

But before speaking of the Roman incorporation of Gaul we must notice that in the hundred years after the final fall of Carthage, the Eastern Mediterranean had also begun to come into line. This Western power, the Roman, thus finally established, occupied Corinth in the same decade as that which saw the final destruction of Carthage, and what had once been Greece became a Roman province. All the Alexandrian or Grecian East—Syria, Egypt—followed. The Macedonian power in its provinces came to depend upon the Roman system in a series of protectorates, annexations, and occupations, which two generations or so before the foundation of the Catholic Church had made Rome, though her system was not yet complete, the center of the whole Mediterranean world. The men whose sons lived to be contemporary with the Nativity saw that the unity of that world was already achieved. The World was now one, and was built up of the islands, the peninsulas, and the littoral of the Inland Sea.

So the Empire might have remained, and so one would think it naturally would have remained, a Mediterranean thing, but for that capital experiment which has determined all future history—Julius Caesar's conquest of Gaul—Gaul, the mass of which lay North, Continental, exterior to the Mediterranean: Gaul which linked up with the Atlantic and the North Sea: Gaul which lived by the tides: Gaul which was to be the foundation of things to come.

It was this experiment—the Roman Conquest of Gaul—and its

success which opened the ancient and immemorial culture of the Mediterranean to the world. It was a revolution which for rapidity and completeness has no parallel. Something less than a hundred small Celtic States, partially civilized (but that in no degree comparable to the high life of the Mediterranean), were occupied, taught, and, as it were, "converted" into citizens of this now united Roman civilization.

It was all done, so to speak, within the lifetime of a man. The link and cornerstone of Western Europe, the quadrilateral which lies between the Pyrenees and the Rhine, between the Mediterranean, the Atlantic, and the Channel, accepted civilization in a manner so final and so immediate that no historian has ever quite been able to explain the phenomenon. Gaul accepted almost at once the Roman language, the Roman food, the Roman dress, and it formed the first—and a gigantic— extension of European culture.

We shall later find Gaul providing the permanent and enduring example of that culture which survived when the Roman system fell into decay. Gaul led to Britain. The Iberian Peninsula, after the hardest struggle which any territory had presented, was also incorporated. By the close of the first century after the Incarnation, when the Catholic Church had already been obscurely founded in many a city, and the turn of the world's history had come, the Roman Empire was finally established in its entirety. By that time, from the Syrian Desert to the Atlantic, from the Sahara to the Irish Sea and to the Scotch hills, to the Rhine and the Danube, in one great ring fence, there lay a secure and unquestioned method of living incorporated as one great State.

This State was to be the soil in which the seed of the Church was to be sown. As the religion of this State the Catholic Church was to develop. This State is still present, underlying our apparently complex political arrangements, as the main rocks of a country underlie the drift of the surface. Its institutions of property and of marriage; its conceptions of law; its literary roots of Rhetoric, of Poetry, of Logic, are still the stuff of Europe. The religion which it made as universal as itself is still, and perhaps more notably than ever, apparent to all.

2

WHAT WAS THE CHURCH
IN THE ROMAN EMPIRE?

So far I have attempted to answer the question, "What Was the Roman Empire?" We have seen that it was an institution of such and such a character, but to this we had to add that it was an institution affected from its origin, and at last permeated by, *another* institution. This other institution had (and has) for its name "The Catholic Church."

My next task must, therefore, be an attempt to answer the question, "What was the Church in the Roman Empire?" for that I have not yet touched.

In order to answer this question we shall do well to put ourselves in the place of a man living in a particular period, from whose standpoint the nature of the connection between the Church and the Empire can best be observed. And that standpoint in time is the generation which lived through the close of the second century and on into the latter half of the third century: say from A.D. 190 to A.D. 270. It is the first moment in which we can perceive the Church as a developed organism now apparent to all.

If we take an earlier date we find ourselves in a world where the growing Church was still but slightly known and by most people unheard of. We can get no earlier view of it as part of the society around it. It is from about this time also that many documents survive. I shall show that the appearance of the Church at this time, from one hundred and fifty to two hundred and forty years after the Crucifixion, is ample evidence of her original constitution.

A man born shortly after the reign of Marcus Aurelius, living through the violent civil wars that succeeded the peace of the Antonines, surviving to witness the Decian persecution of the Church and in extreme old age to perceive the promise, though not the establishment, of an untrammelled Catholicism (it had yet to pass through the last and most terrible of the persecutions), would have been able to answer our question well. He would have lived at the turn of the tide: a witness to the emergence, apparent to all Society, of the Catholic Church.

Let us suppose him the head of a Senatorial family in some great provincial town such as Lyons. He would then find himself one of a comparatively small class of very wealthy men to whom was confined the municipal government of the city. Beneath him he would be accustomed to a large class of citizens, free men but not senatorial; beneath these again his society reposed upon a very large body of slaves.

In what proportion these three classes of society would have been found in a town like Lyons in the second century we have no exact documents to tell us, but we may infer from what we know of that society that the majority would certainly have been of the servile class, free men less numerous, while senators were certainly a very small body (they were the great landowners of the neighborhood); and we must add to these three main divisions two other classes which complicate our view of that society. The first was that of the freed men, the second was made up of perpetual tenants, nominally free, but economically (and already partly in legal theory) bound to the wealthier classes.

The freed men had risen from the servile class by the sole act of their masters. They were bound to these masters very strongly so far as social atmosphere went, and to no small extent in legal theory as well. This preponderance of a small wealthy class we must not look upon as a stationary phenomenon: it was increasing. In another half-dozen generations it was destined to form the outstanding feature of all imperial society. In the fourth and fifth centuries when the Roman Empire became from Pagan, Christian, the mark of the world was the possession of nearly all its soil and capital (apart from public land) by one small body of immensely wealthy men: the product of the pagan Empire.

It is next important to remember that such a man as we are conceiving would never have regarded the legal distinctions between slave and free as a line of cleavage between different kinds of men. It was a social arrangement and no more. Most of the slaves were, indeed, still chattel, bought and sold; many of them were incapable of any true family life. But there was nothing uncommon in a slave being treated as a friend, in his being a member of the liberal professions, in his acting as a tutor, as an administrator of his master's fortune, or a doctor. Certain official things he could not be; he could not hold any public office, of course; he could never plead; and he could not be a soldier.

This last point is essential; because the Roman Empire, though it required no large armed force in comparison with the total numbers of its vast population (for it was not a system of mere repression—no such system has ever endured), yet could only draw that armed force from a restricted portion of the population. In the absence of foreign adventure or Civil Wars, the armies were mainly used as frontier police. Yet, small as they were, it was not easy to obtain the recruitment required. The wealthy citizen we are considering would have been expected to "find" a certain number of recruits for the service of the army. He found them among his bound free tenants and enfranchised slaves; he was increasingly reluctant to find them; and they were increasingly reluctant to serve. Later recruitment was found more and more from the barbarians outside the Empire; and we shall see on a subsequent page how this affected the transition from the ancient world to that of the Dark Ages.

Let us imagine such a man going through the streets of Lyons of a morning to attend a meeting of the Curia. He would salute, and be saluted, as he passed, by many men of the various classes I have described. Some, though slaves, he would greet familiarly; others, though nominally free and belonging to his own following or to that of some friend, he would regard with less attention. He would be accompanied, it may be presumed, by a small retinue, some of whom might be freed men of his own, some slaves, some of the tenant class, some in legal theory quite independent of him and yet by the economic necessities of the moment practically his dependents.

As he passes through the streets he notes the temples dedicated to a variety of services. No creed dominated the city; even the local gods were now but a confused memory; a religious ritual of the official type was to greet him upon his entry to the Assembly, but in the public life of the city no fixed philosophy, no general faith, appeared.

Among the many buildings so dedicated, two perhaps would have struck his attention: the one the great and showy synagogue where the local Jews met upon their Sabbath, the other a small Christian Church. The first of these he would look on as one looks today upon the mark of an alien colony in some great modern city. He knew it to be the symbol of a small, reserved, unsympathetic but wealthy race scattered throughout the Empire. The Empire had had trouble with it in the past, but that trouble was long forgotten; the little colonies of Jews had become negotiators, highly separate from their fellow citizens, already unpopular, but nothing more.

With the Christian Church it would be otherwise. He would know as an administrator (we will suppose him a pagan) that this Church was *endowed*; that it was possessed of property more or less legally guaranteed. It had a very definite position of its own among the congregations and corporations of the city, peculiar, and yet well secured. He would further know as an administrator (and this would more concern him—for the possession of property by so important a body would seem natural enough), that to this building and the corporation of which it was a symbol were attached an appreciable number of his fellow citizens; a small minority, of course, in any town of such a date (the first generation of the third century), but a minority most appreciable and most worthy of his concern from three very definite characteristics. In the first place it was certainly growing; in the second place it was certainly, even after so many generations of growth, a phenomenon perpetually novel; in the third place (and this was the capital point) it represented a true political organism—

the only subsidiary organism which had risen within the general body of the Empire.

If the reader will retain no other one of the points I am making in this description, let him retain this point: it is, from the historical point of view, the explanation of all that was to follow. The Catholic Church in Lyons would have been for that Senator a distinct organism; with its own officers, its own peculiar spirit, its own type of vitality, which, if he were a wise man, he would know was certain to endure and to grow, and which even if he were but a superficial and unintelligent spectator, he would recognize as unique.

Like a sort of little State the Catholic Church included all classes and kinds of men, and like the Empire itself, within which it was growing, it regarded all classes of its own members as subject to it within its own sphere. The senator, the tenant, the freed man, the slave, the soldier, insofar as they were members of this corporation, were equally bound to certain observances. *Did they neglect these observances, the corporation would expel them or subject them to penalties of its own.* He knew that though misunderstandings and fables existed with regard to this body, there was no social class in which its members had not propagated a knowledge of its customs. He knew (and it would disturb him to know) that its organization, though in no way admitted by law, and purely what we should call "voluntary," was strict and very formidable.

Here in Lyons as elsewhere, it was under a monarchial head called by the Greek name of *Episcopos.* Greek was a language which the cultured knew and used throughout the western or Latin part of the Empire to which he belonged; the title would not, therefore, seem to him alien any more than would be the Greek title of *Presbyter*—the name of the official priests acting under this monarchical head of the organization—or than would the Greek title *Diaconos,* which title was attached to an order, just below the priests, which was comprised of the inferior officials of the clerical body.

He knew that this particular cult, like the innumerable others that were represented by the various sacred buildings of the city, had its mysteries, its solemn ritual, and so forth, in which these, the officials of its body, might alone engage, and which the mass of the local "Christians"—for such was their popular name— attended as a congregation. But he would further know that this scheme of worship differed wholly from any other of the many observances round it *by a certain fixity of definition.* The Catholic Church was not an opinion, nor a fashion, nor a philosophy; it was not a theory nor a habit; it was a *clearly delineated body corporate based on numerous exact doctrines,* extremely jealous of its unity and of its precise definitions, and filled, as was no other body of men at that time, with passionate conviction.

By this I do not mean that the Senator so walking to his official duties could not have recalled from among his own friends more than one who was attached to the Christian body in a negligent sort of way, perhaps by the influence of his wife, perhaps by a tradition inherited from his father: he would guess, and justly guess, that this rapidly growing body counted very many members who were indifferent and some, perhaps, who were ignorant of its full doctrine. But the body as a whole, in its general spirit, and *especially in the disciplined organization of its hierarchy,* did differ from everything round it in this double character of precision and conviction. There was no certitude left and no definite spirit or mental aim, no "dogma" (as we should say today) taken for granted in the Lyons of his time, save among the Christians.

The pagan masses were attached, without definite religion, to a number of customs. In social morals they were guided by certain institutions, at the foundation of which were the Roman ideas of property in men, land and goods; patriotism, the bond of smaller societies, had long ago merged in the conception of a universal empire. This Christian Church alone represented a complete theory of life, to which men were attached, as they had hundreds of years before been attached to their local city, with its local gods and intense corporate local life.

Without any doubt the presence of that Church and of what it stood for would have concerned our Senator. It was no longer negligible nor a thing to be only occasionally observed. It was a permanent force and, what is more, a State within the State.

If he were like most of his kind in that generation, the Catholic Church would have affected him as an irritant; its existence interfered with the general routine of public affairs. If he were, as a small minority even of the rich already were, in sympathy with it though not of it, it would still have concerned him. It was the only exceptional organism of his uniform time: and it was growing.

This Senator goes into the Curia. He deals with the business of the day. It includes complaints upon certain assessments of the Imperial taxes. He consults the lists and sees there (it was the fundamental conception of the whole of that society) men drawn up in grades of importance exactly corresponding to the amount of freehold land which each possessed. He has to vote, perhaps, upon some question of local repairs, the making of some new street, or the establishment of some monument. Probably he hears of some local quarrel provoked (he is told) by the small, segregated Christian body, and he follows the police report upon it.

He leaves the Curia for his own business and hears at home the accounts of his many farms, what deaths of slaves there have been, what has been the result of the harvest, what purchases of slaves or goods have been made, what difficulty there has been in recruiting among his tenantry for the army, and so forth. Such a man was concerned one way or another with perhaps a dozen large farming centers or villages, and had some thousands of human beings dependent upon him. In this domestic business he hardly comes across the Church at all. It was still in the towns. It was not yet rooted in the countryside.

There might possibly, even at that distance from the frontiers, be rumors of some little incursion or other of barbarians; perhaps a few hundred fighting men, come from the outer Germanies, had taken refuge with a Roman garrison after suffering defeat at the hands of neighboring barbarians; or perhaps they were attempting to live by pillage in the neighborhood of the garrison and the soldiers had been called out against them. He might have, from the hands of a friend in that garrison, a letter brought to him officially by the imperial post, which was organized along all the great highways, telling him what had been done to the marauders or the suppliants; how, too, some had, after capture, been allotted land to till under conditions nearly servile, others, perhaps, forcibly recruited for the army. The news would never for a moment have suggested to him any coming danger to the society in which he lived.

He would have passed from such affairs to recreations probably literary, and there would have been an end of his day.

In such a day what we note as most exceptional is the aspect of the small Catholic body in a then pagan city, and we should remember, if we are to understand history, that by this time it was already the phenomenon which contemporaries were also beginning to note most carefully.

That is a fair presentment of the manner in which a number of local affairs (including the Catholic Church in his city) would have struck such a man at such a time.

If we use our knowledge to consider the Empire as a whole, we must observe certain other things in the landscape, touching the Church and the society around it, which a local view cannot give us. In the first place there had been in that society from time to time acute spasmodic friction breaking out between the Imperial power and this separate voluntary organism, the Catholic Church. The Church's partial secrecy, its high vitality, its claim to independent administration, were the superficial causes of this. Speaking as Catholics, we know that the ultimate causes were more profound. The conflict was a conflict between Jesus Christ with His great foundation on the one hand, and what Jesus Christ Himself had called "the world." But it is unhistorical to think of a "Pagan" world opposed to a "Christian" world at that time. The very conception of "a Pagan world" requires some external manifest Christian civilization against which to contrast it. There was none such, of course, for Rome in the first generation of the third century. The Church had around her a society in which education was very widely spread, intellectual curiosity very lively, a society largely skeptical, but interested to discover the right conduct of human life, and tasting now this opinion, now that, to see if it could discover a final solution.

It was a society of such individual freedom that it is difficult to speak of its "luxury" or its "cruelty." A cruel man could be cruel in it without suffering the punishment which centuries of Christian training would render natural to our ideas. But a merciful man could be, and would be, merciful and would preach mercy, and would be generally applauded. It was a society in which there were many ascetics—whole schools of thought contemptuous of sensual pleasure—but a society distinguished from the Christian particularly in this, that at bottom it *believed man to be sufficient to himself and all belief to be mere opinions.*

Here was the great antithesis between the Church and her surroundings. It is an antithesis which has been revived today. Today, outside the Catholic Church, there is no distinction between opinion and faith nor any idea that man is other than sufficient to himself.

The Church did not, and does not, believe man to be sufficient to himself, nor naturally in possession of those keys which would open the doors to full knowledge or full social content. It proposed (and proposes) its doctrines to be held not as opinions but as a body of faith.

It differed from—or was more solid than—all around it in this: that it proposed statement instead of hypothesis, affirmed concrete historical facts instead of suggesting myths, and treated its ritual of "mysteries" as realities instead of symbols.

A word as to the constitution of the Church. All men with an historical training know that the Church of the years 200-250 was what I have described it, an organized society under bishops, and, what is more, it is evident that there was a central primacy at Rome as well as local primacies in various other great cities. But what is not so generally emphasized is the way in which Christian society appears to have *looked at itself* at that time.

The conception which the Catholic Church had of *itself* in the early third century can, perhaps, best be approached by pointing out that if we use the word "Christianity" we are unhistorical. "Christianity" is a term in the mouth and upon the pen of the post-Reformation writer; it connotes an opinion or a theory; a point of view; an idea. The Christians of the time of which I speak had no such conception. Upon the contrary, they were attached to its very antithesis. They were attached to the conception of a *thing*: of an organized body instituted for a definite end, disciplined in a definite way, and remarkable for the possession of definite and concrete doctrine. One can talk, in speaking of the first three centuries, of stoic*ism*, or epicurean*ism*, or neoplaton*ism*; but one cannot talk of "Christian*ism*" or "Christ*ism*." Indeed, no one has been so ignorant or unhistorical as to attempt those phrases. But the current phrase "Christianity," used by moderns as identical with the Christian body in the third century, is intellectually the equivalent of "Christianism" or "Christism"; and, I repeat, it connotes a grossly unhistorical idea; it connotes something historically false; something that never existed.

Let me give an example of what I mean:

Four men will be sitting as guests of a fifth in a private house in Carthage in the year 225. They are all men of culture; all possessed of the two languages, Greek and Latin, well-read and interested in the problems and half-solutions of their skeptical time. One will profess himself Materialist, and will find another to agree with him; there is no personal God, certain moral duties must be recognized by men for such and such utilitarian reasons, and so forth. He finds support.

The host is not of that opinion; he has been profoundly influenced by certain "mysteries" into which he has been "initiated": That is, symbolical plays showing the fate of the soul and performed in high seclusion before members of a society sworn to secrecy. He has come to feel a spiritual life as the natural life round him. He has curiously followed, and often paid at high expense, the services of necromancers; he believes that in an "initiation" which he experienced in his youth, and during the secret and most vivid drama or "mystery" in which he then took part, he actually came in contact with the spiritual world. Such men were not uncommon. The declining society of the time was already turning to influences of that type.

The host's conviction, his awed and reticent attitude towards such things, impress his guests. One of the guests, however, a simple, solid kind of man, not drawn to such vagaries, says that he has been reading with great interest the literature of the Christians. He is in admiration of the traditional figure of the Founder of their Church. He quotes certain phrases, especially from the four orthodox Gospels. They move him to eloquence, and their poignancy and illuminative power have an effect upon his friends. He ends by saying: "For my part, I have come to make it a sort of rule to act as this Man Christ would have had me act. He seems to me to have led the most perfect life I ever read of, and the practical maxims which are attached to His Name seem to me a sufficient guide to life. That," he will conclude simply, "is the groove into which I have fallen, and I do not think I shall ever leave it."

Let us call the man who has so spoken, Ferreolus. Would Ferreolus have been a *Christian?* Would the officials of the Roman Empire have called him a *Christian?* Would he have been in danger of unpopularity where *Christians* were unpopular? Would *Christians* have received him among themselves as part of their strict and still somewhat secret society? Would he have counted with any single man of the whole Empire as one of the *Christian* body?

The answer is most emphatically *No.*

No Christian in the first three centuries would have held such a man as coming within his view. No imperial officer in the most violent crisis of one of those spasmodic persecutions which the Church had to undergo would have troubled him with a single question. No Christian congregation would have regarded him as in any way connected with their body. Opinion of that sort, "Christism," had no relation to the Church. How far it existed we cannot tell, for it was unimportant. Insofar as it existed it would have been on all fours with any one of the vague opinions which floated about the cultured Roman world.

Now it is evident that the term "Christianity" used as a point of view, a mere mental attitude, would include such a man, and it is equally evident that we have only to imagine him to see that he had nothing to do with the Christian *religion* of that day. For the Christian religion (then as now) was a thing, not a theory. It was expressed in what I have called an organism, and that organism was the Catholic Church.

The reader may here object: "But surely there was heresy after heresy and thousands of men were at any moment claiming the name of Christian whom the orthodox Church rejected. Nay, some suffered martyrdom rather than relinquish the name."

True; but the very existence of such sects should be enough to prove the point at issue.

These sects arose precisely because within the Catholic Church 1) exact doctrine, 2) unbroken tradition, and 3) absolute unity, were, all three, regarded as the necessary marks of the institution. The heresies arose one after another, from the action of men who were prepared to define yet more punctiliously what the truth might be, and to claim with yet more particular insistence the possession of living tradition and the right to be regarded as the center of unity. No heresy pretended that the truth was vague and indefinite. The whole gist and meaning of a heresy was that it, the heresy, or he, the heresiarch, was prepared to make doctrine yet more sharp, and to assert his own definition.

What you find in these foundational times is not the Catholic Church asserting and defining a thing and then, some time after, the heresiarch denying this definition; no heresy comes within a hundred miles of such a procedure. What happens in the early Church is that some doctrine not yet fully defined is laid down by such and such a man, that his final settlement clashes with the opinion of others, that after debate and counsel, and also authoritative statement on the part of the bishops, this man's solution is rejected and an orthodox solution is defined. From that moment the heresiarch, if he will not fall into line with defined opinion, ceases to be in communion; and his rejection, no less than his own original insistence upon his doctrine, are in themselves proofs that both he and his judges postulate unity and definition as the two necessary marks of Catholic truth.

No early heretic or no early orthodox authority dreams of saying to his opponent: "You may be right! Let us agree to differ. Let us each form his part of 'Christian society' and look at things from his own point of view." The moment a question is raised it must of its nature, the early Church being what it was, be defined one way or the other.

Well, then, what was this body of doctrine held by common tradition and present everywhere in the first years of the third century?

Let me briefly set down what we know, as a matter of historical and documentary evidence, the Church of this period to have held. What we know is a very different matter from what we can guess. We may amplify it from our conceptions of the *probable* according to our knowledge of that society—as, for instance, when we say that there was probably a bishop at Marseilles before the middle of the second century. Or we may amplify it by guesswork, and suppose, in the absence of evidence, some just possible but exceedingly improbable thing: as, that an important canonical Gospel has been lost. There is an infinite range for guesswork, both orthodox and heretical. But the plain and known facts which repose upon historical and documentary evidence, and which have no corresponding documentary evidence against them, are both few and certain.

Let us take such a writer as Tertullian and set down what was certainly true of his time.

Tertullian was a man of about forty in the year 200. The Church then taught as an unbroken tradition that a Man who had been put to death about 170 years before in Palestine—only 130 years before Tertullian's birth—had risen again on the third day. This Man was a known and real person with whom numbers had conversed. In Tertullian's childhood men still lived who had met eyewitnesses of the thing asserted.

This Man (the Church said) was also the supreme Creator God. There you have an apparent contradiction in terms, at any rate a mystery, fruitful in opportunities for theory, and as a fact destined to lead to three centuries of more and more particular definition.

This Man, Who also was God Himself, had, through chosen

companions called Apostles, founded a strict and disciplined society called the Church. The doctrines the Church taught professed to be His doctrines. They included the immortality of the human soul, its redemption, its alternative of salvation and damnation.

Initiation into the Church was by way of baptism with water in the name of The Trinity: Father, Son and Holy Ghost.

Before His death this Man Who was also God had instituted a certain rite and *Mystery* called the Eucharist. He took bread and wine and changed them into His Body and Blood. He ordered this rite to be continued. The central act of worship of the Christian Church was therefore a consecration of bread and wine by priests in the presence of the initiated and baptized Christian body of the locality. The bread and wine so consecrated were certainly called (universally) the Body of the Lord.

The faithful also certainly communicated, that is, ate the Bread and drank the Wine thus changed in the *Mystery*.

It was the central rite of the Church thus to [offer to God the Father and to] take the Body of the Lord.

There was certainly at the head of each Christian community a bishop: regarded as directly the successor of the Apostles, the chief agent of the ritual and the guardian of doctrine.

The whole increasing body of local communities kept in touch through their bishops, held one doctrine and practiced what was substantially one ritual.

All that is plain history.

The numerical proportion of the Church in the city of Carthage, where Tertullian wrote, was certainly large enough for its general suppression to be impossible. One might argue from one of his phrases that it was a tenth of the population. Equally certainly did the unity of the Christian Church and its bishops teach the institution of the Eucharist, the Resurrection, the authority of the Apostles, and their power of tradition through the bishops. A very large number of converts were to be noted and (to go back to Tertullian) the majority of his time, by his testimony, were recruited by conversion, and were not born Christians.

Such is known to have been, in a very brief outline, the manner of the Catholic Church in these early years of the third century. Such was the undisputed manner of the Church, as a Christian or an inquiring pagan would have been acquainted with it in the years 160-200 and onwards.

I have purposely chosen this moment, because it is the moment in which Christian evidence first emerges upon any considerable scale. Many of the points I have set down are, of course, *demonstrably* anterior to the third century. I mean by "demonstrably" anterior, proved in earlier documentary testimony. That ritual and doctrine firmly fixed are long anterior to the time in which you find them rooted is obvious to common sense. But there are documents as well.

Thus, we have Justin Martyr. He was no less than sixty years older than Tertullian. He was as near to the Crucifixion as my generation is to the Reform Bill—and he gave us a full description of the Mass.

We have the letters of St. Ignatius. He was a much older man than St. Justin—perhaps forty or fifty years older. He stood to the generations contemporary with Our Lord as I stand to the generation of Gladstone, Bismarck, and, early as he is, he testifies fully to the organization of the Church with its Bishops, the Eucharistic Doctrine, and the Primacy in it of the Roman See.

The literature remaining to us from the early first century and a half after the Crucifixion is very scanty. The writings of what are called "Apostolic" times—that is, documents proceeding immediately from men who could remember the time of Our Lord, form not only in their quantity (and that is sufficiently remarkable), but in their quality, too, a far superior body of evidence to what we possess from the next generation. We have more in the New Testament than we have in the writings of these men who came just after the death of the Apostles. But what does remain is quite convincing. There arose from the date of Our Lord's Ascension into heaven, from, say, A.D. 30 or so, before the death of Tiberius and a long lifetime after the Roman organization of Gaul, a definite, strictly ruled and highly individual *Society*, with fixed doctrines, special mysteries, and a strong discipline of its own. With a most vivid and distinct personality, unmistakable. And this Society was, and is, called "The Church."

I would beg the reader to note with precision both the task upon which we are engaged and the exact dates with which we are dealing, for there is no matter in which history has been more grievously distorted by religious bias.

The task upon which we are engaged is the judgment of a portion of history as it was. I am not writing here from a brief. I am concerned to set forth a fact. I am acting as a witness or a copier, not as an advocate or lawyer. And I say that the conclusion we can establish with regard to the Christian community on these main lines is the conclusion to which any man must come quite independently of his creed. He will deny these facts only if he has such bias against the Faith as interferes with his reason. A man's belief in the mission of the Catholic Church, his confidence in its divine origin, do not move him to these plain historical conclusions any more than they move him to his conclusions upon the real existence, doctrine and organization of contemporary Mormonism. Whether the Church told the truth is for philosophy to discuss: What the Church in fact *was* is plain history. The Church may have taught nonsense. Its organization may have been a clumsy human thing. That would not affect the historical facts.

By the year 200 the Church was—everywhere, manifestly and in ample evidence throughout the Roman world—what I have described, and taught the doctrines I have just enumerated: but it stretches back one hundred and seventy years before that date and it has evidence to its title throughout that era of youth.

To see that the state of affairs everywhere widely apparent in A.D. 200 was rooted in the very origins of the institution one hundred and seventy years before, to see that all this mass of ritual, doctrine and discipline starts with the first third of the first century, and the Church was from its birth the Church, the reader must consider the dates.

We know that we have in the body of documents contained

in the "canon" which the Church has authorized as the "New Testament," documents proceeding from men who were contemporaries with the origin of the Christian religion. Even modern scholarship with all its love of phantasy is now clear upon so obvious a point. The authors of the Gospels, the Acts, and the Epistles, Clement also, and [St.] Ignatius [of Antioch] also (who had conversed with the Apostles) may have been deceived, they may have been deceiving. I am not here concerned with that point. The discussion of it belongs to another province of argument altogether. But they were *contemporaries* of the things they said they were contemporaries of. In other words, their writings are what is called "authentic."

If I read in the four Gospels (not only the first three) of such and such a miracle, I believe it or I disbelieve it. But I am reading the account of a man who lived at the time when the miracle is *said* to have happened. If you read (in Ignatius' seven certainly genuine letters) of Episcopacy and of the Eucharist, you may think him a wrong-headed enthusiast. But you know that you are reading the work of a man who *personally* witnessed the beginnings of the Church; you know that the customs, manners, doctrines and institutions he mentions or takes for granted were certainly those of his time, that is, of the *origin* of Catholicism, though you may think the customs silly and the doctrines nonsense.

St. Ignatius talking about the origin and present character of the Catholic Church is exactly in the position—in the matter of dates—of a man of our time talking about the rise and present character of the Socialists or of the rise and present character of Leopold's Kingdom of Belgium, of United Italy, the modern. He is talking of what is, virtually, his own time.

Well, there comes after this considerable body of *contemporary* documentary evidence (evidence contemporary, that is, with the very spring and rising of the Church and proceeding from its first founders), a gap which is somewhat more than the long lifetime of a man.

This gap is with difficulty bridged. The vast mass of its documentary evidence has, of course, perished, as has the vast mass of all ancient writing. The little preserved is mainly preserved in quotations and fragments. But after this gap, from somewhat before the year 200, we come to the beginning of a regular series, and a series increasing in volume, of documentary evidence. Not, I repeat, of evidence to the *truth* of supernatural doctrines, but of evidence to what these doctrines and their accompanying ritual and organization were: evidence to the way in which the Church was constituted, to the way in which she regarded her mission, to the things she thought important, to the practice of her rites.

That is why I have taken the early third century as the moment in which we can first take a full historical view of the Catholic Church in being, and this picture is full of evidence to the state of the Church in its origins three generations before.

I say, again, it is all-important for the reader who desires a true historical picture to seize the *sequence of the dates with which we are dealing,* their relation to the length of human life and therefore to the society to which they relate.

It is all-important because the false history which has had its own way for so many years is based upon two false suggestions of the first magnitude. The first is the suggestion that the period between the Crucifixion and the full Church of the third century was one in which vast changes could proceed unobserved, and vast perversions of original ideas be rapidly developed; the second is that the space of time during which those changes are supposed to have taken place was sufficient to account for them.

It is only because those days are remote from ours that such suggestions can be made. If we put ourselves by an effort of the imagination into the surroundings of that period, we can soon discover how false these suggestions are.

The period was not one favorable to the interruption of record. It was one of a very high culture. The proportion of curious, intellectual, and skeptical men which that society contained was perhaps greater than in any other period with which we are acquainted. It was certainly greater than it is today. Those times were certainly less susceptible to mere novel assertion than are the crowds of our great cities under the influence of the modern press. It was a period astonishingly alive. Lethargy and decay had not yet touched the world of the Empire. It built, read, traveled, discussed, and, above all, *criticized,* with an enormous energy.

In general, it was no period during which alien fashions could rise within such a community as the Church without their opponents being immediately able to combat them by an appeal to the evidence of the immediate past. The world in which the Church arose was one; and that world was intensely vivid. Anyone in that world who saw such an institution as Episcopacy (for instance) or such a doctrine as the Divinity of Christ to be a novel corruption of originals could have, and would have, protested at once. It was a world of ample record and continual communication.

Granted such a world, let us take the second point and see what was the distance in mere time between this early third century of which I speak and what is called the Apostolic period; that is, the generation which could still remember the origins of the Church in Jerusalem and the preaching of the Gospel in Grecian, Italian, and perhaps African cities. We are often told that changes "gradually crept in," that "the imperceptible effect of time" did this or that. Let us see how these vague phrases stand the test of confrontation with actual dates.

Let us stand in the years 200-210; consider a man then advanced in years, well read and traveled, and present in those first years of the third century at the celebration of the Eucharist. There were many such men who, if they had been able to do so, would have reproved novelties and denounced perverted tradition. That none did so is a sufficient proof that the main lines of Catholic government and practice had developed unbroken and unwarped from at least his own childhood. But an old man who so witnessed the constitution of the Church and its practices as I have described them in the year 200, would correspond to that generation of old people whom we have with us today; the old people who were born in the late twenties and thirties of the nineteenth century; the old people who can just remember the English Reform Bill, and who were almost grown up during the troubles of 1848 and the establishment of the second Empire in Paris: the old people in the United States who can remember as children the election of Van Buren to the office of President: the old people whose birth was not far removed from the death of Thomas Jefferson, and who were grown men and women when gold was first discovered in California.

Well, pursuing that parallel, consider next the persecution under Nero. It was the great event to which the Christians would refer as a date in the early history of the Church. It took place in Apostolic times. It affected men who, though aged, could easily remember Judea in the years connected with Our Lord's mission and His Passion. St. Peter lived to witness, in that persecution, to the Faith. St. John survived it. It came not forty years later than the day of Pentecost. But the persecution under Nero was to an old man such as I have supposed assisting at the Eucharist in the early part of the third century, no further off than the Declaration of Independence is from the old people of our generation. An old man in the year 200 could certainly remember many who had themselves been witnesses of the Apostolic age, just as an old man today remembers well men who saw the French Revolution and the Napoleonic wars. The old people who had surrounded his childhood would be to St. Paul, St. Peter and St. John what the old people who survived, say, to 1845, would have been to Jefferson, to Lafayette, or to the younger Pitt. They could have seen and talked to that first generation of the Church as the corresponding people surviving in the early nineteenth century could have seen and talked with the founders of the United States.

It is quite impossible to imagine that the Eucharistic Sacrifice, the Rite of Initiation (Baptism in the name of the Trinity), the establishment of an Episcopacy, the fierce defence of unity and orthodoxy, and all those main lines of Catholicism which we find to be the very essence of the Church in the early third century, could have risen without protest. They cannot have come from an innocent, natural, uncivilized perversion of an original so very recent and so open to every form of examination.

That there should have been discussion as to the definition

and meaning of undecided [i.e., undefined] doctrines is natural, and fits in both with the dates and with the atmosphere of the period and with the character of the subject. But that a whole scheme of Christian government and doctrine should have developed in contradiction of Christian origins and yet without protest in a period so brilliantly living, full of such rapid intercommunication, and, *above all, so brief,* is quite impossible.

That is what history has to say of the early Church in the Roman Empire. The Gospels, the Acts, the canonical Epistles and those of Clement and Ignatius may tell a true or a false story; their authors may have written under an illusion or from a conscious self-deception; or they may have been supremely true and immutably sincere. *But they are contemporary.* A man may respect their divine origin or he may despise their claims to instruct the human race; but that the Christian body from its beginning was not "Christianity" but a Church and that that Church was identically one with what was already called long before the third century[1] the *Catholic* Church, is simply plain history, as plain and straightforward as the history, let us say, of municipal institutions in contemporary Gaul. It is history indefinitely better proved, and therefore indefinitely more certain than, let us say, modern guesswork on imaginary "Teutonic Institutions" before the eighth century or the still more imaginary "Aryan" origins of the European race, or any other of the pseudo-scientific hypotheses which still try to pass for historical truth.

So much for the Catholic Church in the early third century when first we have a mass of evidence upon it. It is a highly disciplined, powerful growing body, intent on unity, ruled by bishops, having for its central doctrine the Incarnation of God in an historical Person, Jesus Christ, and for its central rite a Mystery, the transformation of bread and wine by priests into the Body and Blood which the faithful consume.

---

1. The Muratorian Fragment is older than the third century, and St. Ignatius, who also uses the word Catholic, was as near to the time of the Gospels as I am to the Crimean War.

This "State within the States" by the year 200 already had affected the Empire: in the next generation it permeated the Empire; it was already transforming European civilization. By the year 200 the thing was done. As the Empire declined, the Catholic Church caught and preserved it.

What was the process of that decline?

To answer such a question we have next to observe three developments that followed: 1) The great increase of barbarian hired soldiery within the Empire; 2) The weakening of the central power as compared with the local power of the small and increasingly rich class of great landowners; 3) The rise of the Catholic Church from an admitted position (and soon a predominating position) to complete mastery over all society.

All these three phenomena developed together; they occupied about two hundred years—roughly from the year 300 to the year 500. When they had run their course the Western Empire was no longer governed as one society from one Imperial center. The chance heads of certain auxiliary forces in the Roman Army, drawn from barbaric recruitment, had established themselves in the various provinces and were calling themselves "Kings." The Catholic Church was everywhere the religion of the great majority; it had everywhere alliance with, and often the use of, the official machinery of government and taxation, which continued unbroken. It had become, far beyond all other organisms in the Roman State, the central and typical organism which gave the European world its note. This process is commonly called "The Fall of the Roman Empire"; what was that "fall"? What really happened in this great transformation?

3

WHAT WAS THE "FALL" OF
THE ROMAN EMPIRE?

That state of society which I have just described, the ordered and united society of the Roman Empire, passed into another and very different state of society: the society of what are called "The Dark Ages."

From these again rose, after another 600 years of adventures and perils, the great harvest of mediaeval civilization. Hardly had the Roman Empire turned in its maturity to accept the fruit of its long development (I mean the Catholic Church), when it began to grow old and was clearly about to suffer some great transition. But that transition, which threatened to be death, proved in the issue not death at all, but a mixture of Vision and Change.

The close succession of fruit and decay in society is what one expects from the analogy of all living things: at the close of the cycle it is death that should come. A plant, just after it is most fruitful, falls quickly. So, one might imagine, should the long story of Mediterranean civilization have proceeded. When it was at its final and most complete stage, one would expect some final and complete religion which should satisfy its long search and solve its ancient riddles: but after such a discovery, after the fruit of such a maturity had fully developed, one would expect an end.

Now it has been the singular fortune of our European civilization that an end did not come. Dissolution was in some strange way checked. Death was averted. And the more closely one looks into the unique history of that salvation—the salvation of

all that could be saved in a most ancient and fatigued society—
the more one sees that this salvation was effected by no agency
save that of the Catholic Church. Everything else, after, say, 250
A.D., the empty fashionable philosophies, the barbarians filling
the army, the current passions and the current despair, made for
nothing but ruin.

There is no parallel to this survival in all the history of mankind. Every other great civilization has, after many centuries
of development, either fallen into a fixed and sterile sameness
or died and disappeared. There is nothing left of Egypt, there
is nothing left of Assyria. The Eastern civilizations remain, but
remain immovable; or if they change can only vulgarly copy
external models.

But the civilization of Europe—the civilization, that is, of
Rome and of the Empire—had a third fortune differing both from
death and from sterility: it survived to a resurrection. Its essential seeds were preserved for a Second Spring.

For five or six hundred years men carved less well, wrote
verse less well, let roads fall slowly into ruin, lost or rather
coarsened the machinery of government, forgot or neglected
much in letters and in the arts and in the sciences. But there
was preserved, right through that long period, not only so much
of letters and of the arts as would suffice to bridge the great
gulf between the fifth century and the eleventh, but also so much
of what was really vital in the mind of Europe as would permit
that mind to blossom again after its repose. And the agency, I
repeat, which effected this conservation of the seeds, was the
Catholic Church.

It is impossible to understand this truth, indeed it is impossible
to make any sense at all of European history, if we accept that
story of the decline which is currently put forward in anti-
Catholic academies, and which has seemed sufficient to anti-
Catholic historians.

Their version is, briefly, this: The Roman Empire, becoming
corrupt and more vicious through the spread of luxury and
through a sort of native weakness to be discovered in the very
blood of the Mediterranean, was at last invaded and over-

whelmed by young and vigorous tribes of Germans. These brought with them all the strength of those native virtues which later rejected the unity of Christendom and began the modern Protestant societies—which are already nearly atheist and very soon will be wholly so.

A generic term has been invented by these modern and false historians whose version I am here giving; the vigorous, young, uncorrupt, and virtuous tribes which are imagined to have broken through the boundaries of the effete Empire and to have rejuvenated it, are grouped together as "Teutonic": a German strain very strong numerically, superior also to what was left of Roman civilization in virile power, is said to have come in and to have taken over the handling of affairs. One great body of these Germans, the Franks, are said to have taken over Gaul; another (the Goths, in their various branches) Italy and Spain. But most complete, most fruitful, and most satisfactory of all (they tell us) was the eruption of these vigorous and healthy pagans into the outlying province of Britain, which they wholly conquered, exterminating its original inhabitants and colonizing it with their superior stock.

"It was inevitable" (the anti-Catholic historian proceeds to admit) "that the presence of uncultured though superior men should accelerate the decline of arts in the society which they thus conquered. It is further to be deplored that their simpler and native virtues were contaminated by the arts of the Roman clergy and that in some measure the official religion of Rome captured their noble souls; for that official religion permitted the poison of the Roman decline to affect all the European mind—even the German mind—for many centuries. But at the same time this evil effect was counter-balanced by the ineradicable strength and virtues of the Northern barbaric blood. This sacred Teutonic blood it was which brought into Western Europe the subtlety of romantic conceptions, the true lyric touch in poetry, the deep reverence which was (till recently) the note of their religion, the love of adventure in which the old civilization was lacking, and a vast respect for women. At the same time their warrior spirit evolved the great structure of feudalism, the chivalric model and the whole military ideal of mediaeval civilization.

"Is it to be wondered at that when great new areas of knowledge were opened up in the later fifteenth century by suddenly expanded travel, by the printing press, and by an unexpected advance in physical science, the emancipation of the European mind should have brought this pure and barbaric stock to its own again?

"In proportion as Teutonic blood was strong, in that proportion was the hierarchy of the Catholic Church and the hold upon men of Catholic tradition shaken in the early sixteenth century; and before that century had closed, the manly stirp [i.e., stock] of North Germany, Holland, Scandinavia and England had developed the Protestant civilization, a society advancing, healthy, and already the master of all rivals; destined soon to be, if it be not already, supreme."

Such is not an exaggerated summary of what the anti-Catholic school of history gave us from German and from English universities (with the partial aid of anti-Catholic academic forces within Catholic countries) during the first two-thirds of the nineteenth century.

There went with this strange way of rewriting history a flood of wild hypotheses presented as fact. Thus Parliaments (till lately admired) were imagined—and therefore stated—to be Teutonic, non-Roman, therefore non-Catholic in origin. The gradual decline of slavery was attributed to the same miraculous powers in the northern pagans; and in general whatever thing was good in itself or was consonant with modern ideas, was referred back to this original source of good in the business of Europe: the German tribes.

Meanwhile the religious hatred these false historians had of civilization, that is, of Roman tradition and the Church, showed itself in a hundred other ways: the conquest of Spain by the Mohammedans was represented by them as the victory of a superior people over a degraded and contemptible one: the Reconquest of Spain by our race over the Asiatics as a disaster: its final triumphant instrument, the Inquisition, which saved

Spain from a Moorish ravage was made out a monstrosity. Every revolt, however obscure, against the unity of European civilization in the Middle Ages (notably the worst revolt of all, the Albigensian) was presented as a worthy uplifting of the human mind against conditions of bondage. Most remarkable of all, the actual daily life of Catholic Europe, the habit, way of thought and manner of men during the period of unity—from, say, the eighth century to the fifteenth—was simply omitted!

At the moment when history was struggling to become a scientific study, this school of self-pleasing fairy tales held the field. When at last history *did* become a true scientific study, this school collapsed. But it yet retains, as an inheritance from its old hegemony, a singular power in the lower and more popular forms of historical writing; and where the English language is spoken it is, even today, almost the only view of European development which the general student can obtain.

It will be noted at the outset that the whole of the fantastic picture which this old and now discredited theory presented is based upon a certain conception of what happened at the breakdown of the Roman Empire.

Unless these barbaric German tribes *did* come in and administrate, unless they really *were* very considerable in number, unless their character in truth *was* what this school postulated it to be—vigorous, young, virtuous and all the rest of it—unless there *did indeed* take place a struggle between this imaginary great German nation and the Mediterranean civilization, in which the former won and ruled as conquerors over subject peoples; unless these primary axioms have some historical truth in them, the theory which is deduced from them has no historical value whatsoever.

A man may have a preference, as a Protestant or merely as an inhabitant of North Germany or Scandinavia, for the type of man who originally lived his degraded life outside the Roman Empire. He may, as an anti-Catholic of any kind, hope that civilization was decadent through Catholicism at the end of the united Roman Empire, and it may please him to imagine that the coincidence of what was originally barbaric with what is now Protestant German Europe is a proof of the former's original prowess. Nay, he may even desire that the non-Catholic and non-traditional type in our civilization shall attain to a supremacy which it certainly has not yet reached.[2] But the whole thing is only a pleasant (or unpleasant) dream, something to imagine and not something to discover, unless we have a solid historical foundation for the theory: to wit, the destruction of the Roman Empire in the way which, and by the men whom, the theory presupposes.

The validity of the whole scheme depends upon our answer to the question, "What was the fall of the Roman Empire?"

If it was a conquest such as we have just seen postulated, and a conquest actuated by the motives of men so described, then this old anti-Catholic school, though it could not maintain its exaggerations (though, for instance, it could not connect representative institutions with the German barbarians), would yet be substantially true.

Now the moment documents began to be seriously examined and compared, the moment modern research began to approach some sort of finality in the study of that period wherein the United Roman Empire of the West was replaced by sundry local Kingdoms, students of history thenceforward (and in proportion to their impartiality) became more and more convinced that the whole of this anti-Catholic attitude reposed upon nothing more than assertion.

There was no conquest of effete Mediterranean peoples by vigorous barbarians. The vast number of barbarians who lived as slaves within the Empire, the far smaller number who were pressed or hired into the military service of the Empire, the still smaller number which entered the Empire as marauders, during the weakness of the Central Government towards its end, were not of the sort which this anti-Catholic theory, mistaking its desires for realities, pre-supposed.

The barbarians were not "Germans" (a term difficult to

---

2. I wrote that phrase before the breakup of Prussia and at a moment when Prussia was still the idol of Oxford.

define), they were of very mixed stocks which, if we go by speech (a bad guide to race) were some of them Germanic, some Slav, some even Mongol, some Berber, some of the old unnamed races: the Picts, for instance, and the dark men of the extreme North and West.

They had no conspicuous respect for women of the sort which should produce the chivalric ideal.

They were not free societies, but slave-owning societies.

They did not desire, attempt, or even dream, the destruction of the Imperial power: that misfortune—which was gradual and never complete—insofar as it came about at all, came about in spite of the barbarians and not by their conscious effort.

They were not numerous; on the contrary, they were but handfuls of men, even when they appeared as successful pillagers and raiders over the frontiers. When they came in large numbers, they were wiped out.

They did not introduce any new institutions or any new ideas.

Again, you do not find, in that capital change from the old civilization to the Dark Ages, that the rise of legend and of the romantic and adventurous spirit (the sowing of the modern seed) coincides with places where the great mass of barbaric slaves are settled, or where the fewer barbaric pillagers or the regular barbaric soldiers in the Roman Army pass. Romance appears hundreds of years later, and *it appears more immediately and earliest in connection with precisely those districts in which the passage of the few Teutonic, Slavonic and other barbarians had been least felt.*

There is no link between barbaric society and the feudalism of the Middle Ages; there is no trace of such a link. There is, on the contrary, a very definite and clearly marked historical sequence between Roman civilization and the feudal system, attested by innumerable documents which, once read and compared in their order, leave no sort of doubt that feudalism and the mediaeval civilization repose on purely Roman origins.

In a word, the gradual cessation of central Imperial rule in Western Europe, the failure of the power and habit of one united organization seated in Rome to color, define and administrate the lives of men, was an internal revolution; it did not come from without. It was a change from within; it was nothing remotely resembling an external, still less a barbaric, conquest from without.

All that happened was that Roman civilization, having grown very old, failed to maintain that vigorous and universal method of local government subordinated to the capital which it had for four or five hundred years supported. The machinery of taxation gradually weakened; the whole of central bureaucratic action weakened; the greater men in each locality began to acquire a sort of independence, and sundry soldiers benefited by the slow (and enormous) change, occupied the local "palaces" as they were called, of Roman administration, secured such revenues as the remains of Roman taxation could give them, and, conversely, had thrust upon them so much of the duty of government as the decline of civilization could still maintain. That is what happened, and that is all that happened.

As an historical phenomenon it is what I have called it— enormous. It most vividly struck the imagination of men. The tremors and the occasional local cataclysms which were the symptoms of this change of base from the old high civilization to the Dark Ages, singularly impressed the numerous and prolific writers of the time. Their terrors, their astonishment, their speculations as to the result, have come down to us highly emphasized. We feel after all those centuries the shock which was produced on the literary world of the day by Alaric's sack of Rome, or by the march of the Roman auxiliary troops called "Visigoths" through Gaul into Spain, or by the appearance of the mixed horde called—after their leaders—"Vandals" in front of Hippo in Africa. But what we do *not* feel, what we do *not* obtain from the contemporary documents, what was a mere figment of the academic brain in the generation now just passing away, is that anti-Catholic and anti-civilized bias which would represent the ancient civilization as conquered by men of another and of a better stock who have since developed the supreme type of modern civilization, and whose contrast with the Catholic world and Catholic tradition is at once applauded as the principle of life in Europe and emphasized as the fundamental fact in European history.

The reader will not be content with a mere affirmation, though the affirmation is based upon all that is worth counting in modern scholarship. He will ask what, then, did really happen? After all, Alaric did sack Rome. The Kings of the Franks were Belgian chieftains, probably speaking (at first) Flemish as well as Latin. Those of the Burgundians were probably men who spoke that hotch-potch of original barbaric, Celtic and Roman words later called "Teutonic dialects," as well as Latin. The military officers called (from the original recruitment of their commands) "Goths," both eastern and western, were in the same case. Even that mixed mass of Slav, Berber, escaped slaves and the rest which, from original leaders, was called in North Africa "Vandal," probably had some considerable German nucleus.

The false history has got superficial ground to work upon. Many families whose origins came from what is now German-speaking Central Europe ruled in local government during the transition, and distinct though small tribes, mainly German in speech, survived for a short time in the Empire. Like all false-hood, the falsehood of the "Teutonic theory" could not live without an element of truth to distort, and it is the business of anyone who is writing true history, even in so short an essay as this, to show what that ground was and how it has been mis-represented.

In order to understand what happened we must first of all clearly represent to ourselves the fact that the structure upon which our united civilization had in its first five centuries reposed was the *Roman Army*. By which I do not mean that the number of soldiers was very large compared with the civilian population, but that the organ which was vital in the State, the thing that really counted, the institution upon which men's minds turned, and which they thought of as the foundation of all, was the military institution.

The original city-state of the Mediterranean broke down a little before the beginning of our era.

When (as always ultimately happens in a complex civilization of many millions) self-government had broken down, and when it was necessary, after the desperate faction fights which that breakdown had produced, to establish a strong center of authority, the obvious and, as it were, necessary person to exercise that authority (in a State constituted as was the Roman State) was the Commander-in-Chief of the army; all that the word "Emperor"—the Latin word *Imperator*—means, is a commander-in-chief.

It was the Army which made and unmade Emperors; it was the Army which designed and ordered and even helped to construct the great roads of the Empire. It was in connection with the needs of the Army that those roads were traced. It was the Army which secured (very easily, for peace was popular) the civil order of the vast organism. It was the Army especially which guarded its frontiers against the uncivilized world without; upon the edge of the Sahara and of the Arabian desert; upon the edge of the Scotch mountains; upon the edge of the poor, wild lands between the Rhine and Elbe. On those frontiers the garrisons made a sort of wall within which wealth and right living could accumulate, outside which small and impoverished bodies of men destitute of the arts (notably of writing) save insofar as they rudely copied the Romans or were permeated by adventurous Roman commerce, lived under conditions which, in the Celtic hills, we can partially appreciate from the analogy of ancient Gaul and from tenacious legends, but of which in the German and Slavonic sand-plains, marshes and woods we know hardly anything at all.

Now this main instrument, the Roman Army—the instrument, remember, which not only preserved civil functions, but actually created the master of all civic functions, the Government—went through three very clear stages of change in the first four centuries of the Christian era—up to the year A.D. 400 or so. And it is the transformation of the Roman Army during the first four centuries which explains the otherwise inexplicable change in society just afterwards, in the fifth and sixth centuries—that is, from 400 to 600 A.D.—the turn from the full civilization of Rome to the beginning of the Dark Ages.

In its first stage, during the early Empire, just as the Catholic Church was founded and was beginning to grow, the Roman Army was still theoretically an army of true Roman citizens.[3]

As a matter of fact, the Army was already principally professional, and it was being recruited even in this first stage very largely from the territories Rome had conquered.

Thus we have Caesar raising a Gallic legion almost contemporaneous with his conquest of Gaul. But for a long time after, well into the Christian era, the Army was conceived of in men's minds as a sort of universal institution rooted in the citizenship which men were still proud to claim throughout the Empire, and which belonged only to a minority of its inhabitants; for the majority were slaves.

In the second phase (which corresponded with the beginning of a decline in letters and in the arts, which carries us through the welter of civil wars in the third century and which introduces the remodeled Empire at their close) the Army was becoming purely professional and at the same time drawn from whatever was least fortunate in Roman society. The recruitment of it was treated much after the fashion of a tax; the great landed proprietors (who, by a parallel development in the decline, were becoming the chief economic feature in the Roman State) were summoned to send a certain number of recruits from their estates.

Slaves would often be glad to go, for, hard as were the conditions of military service, it gave them civic freedom, certain honors, a certain pay, and a future for their children. The poorer freed men would also go at the command of their lord (though only of course a certain proportion—for the conscription was very light compared with modern systems, and was made lighter by re-enlistment, long service, absence of reserves, and the use of veterans).

---

3. A soldier was still technically a citizen up to the very end. The conception of a soldier as a citizen, the impossibility, for instance, of his being a slave, was in the very bones of Roman thought. Even when the soldiers were almost entirely recruited from barbarians, that is, from slave stock, the soldiers themselves were free citizens always.

During this second stage, while the Army was becoming less and less civic, and more and more a profession for the destitute and the unfortunate, the unpopularity and the ignorance of military service among the rest of the population was increasing. The average citizen grew more and more divorced from the Army and knew less and less of its conditions. He came to regard it partly as a necessary police force or defense of his frontiers, partly as a nuisance to him at home. He also came to regard it as something with which he had nothing to do. It lived a life separate from himself. It governed (through the power of the Emperor, its chief); it depended on, and also supported or remade, the Imperial Court. But it was external, at the close of the Empire, to general society.

Recruiting was meanwhile becoming difficult, and *the habit grew up of offering the hungry tribes outside the pale of the Empire the advantage of residence within it on condition that they should serve as Roman soldiers.*

The conception of territories within the Empire which were affiliated and allied to it rather than absorbed by it, was a very ancient one. That conception had lost reality so far as the old territories it had once affected were concerned; but it paved the way for the parallel idea of troops affiliated and allied to the Roman Army, part of that army in discipline and organization, yet possessed of considerable freedom within their own divisions.

Here we have not only a constant and increasing use of barbaric troops drafted into the regular corps, but also *whole bodies which were more and more frequently accepted "en bloc" and, under their local leaders, as auxiliaries to the Roman forces.*

Some such bodies appear to have been settled upon land on the frontiers, to others were given similar grants at very great distances from the frontiers. Thus we have a small body of German barbarians settled at Rennes in Brittany. And, again, within the legions (who were all technically of Roman citizenship and in theory recruited from the full civilization of Rome), the barbarian who happened to find himself within that civilization tended more than did his non-barbarian fellow citizen (or fellow slave) to accept military service. He would nearly always be poorer; he would, unless his experience of civilization was a long one, feel the hardship of military service less; and in this second phase, while the army was becoming more sedentary (more attached, that is, to particular garrisons), more permanent, more of an hereditary thing handed on from father to son, and distinguished by the large element of what we call "married quarters," it was also becoming more and more an army of men who, whether as auxiliaries or as true Roman soldiers, were *in blood, descent, and to some extent in manners and less in language, barbarians.* There were negroes, there were probably Celts, there were Slavs, Mongols of the Steppes, more numerous Germans, and so forth.

In the third stage, which is the stage that saw the great convulsion of the fifth century, the army, though not yet wholly barbaric, had already become in its most vital part, barbaric. It took its orders, of course, wholly from the Roman State, but great groups within it were only partly even Latin-speaking or Greek-speaking, and were certainly regarded both by themselves and by their Roman masters as non-Roman in manners and in blood.

It must most clearly be emphasized that not only no such thought as an attack upon the Empire entered the heads of these soldiers, but that the very idea of it would have been inconceivable to them. Had you proposed it they would not even have known what you meant. That a particular section of the army should fight against a particular claimant to the Empire (and therefore and necessarily in favor of some other claimant) they thought natural enough; but to talk of an attack upon the Empire itself would have seemed to them like talking of an attack upon bread and meat, air, water and fire. The Empire was the whole method and meaning of their lives.

At intervals the high and wealthy civilization of the Roman Empire was, of course, subjected to attempted pillage by small and hungry robber bands without its boundaries, but that had nothing to do with the barbaric recruitment of the Roman Army save when such bands were caught and incorporated. The army was always ready at a moment's order to cut such foreign raiders to pieces—and always did so successfully.

The portion of the Army chosen to repel, cut up, and sell into slavery a marauding band of Slavs or Germans or Celts, always had Celts or Slavs or Germans present in large numbers among its own soldiery. But no tie of blood interfered with the business. To consider such a thing would have been inconceivable to the opponents on either side. The distinction was not between speech and speech, still less between vague racial customs. It was a distinction between the Imperial Service on the one side, against the outer, unrecognized, savage on the other.

As the machinery of Government grew weak through old age, and as the recruitment of the Army from barbarians and the large proportion of auxiliary regular forces began to weaken that basis of the whole State, the tendency of pillaging bands to break in past the frontiers into the cultivated lands and the wealth of the cities grew greater and greater; but it never occurred to them to attack the Empire as such. All they wanted was permission to enjoy the life which was led within it, and to abandon the wretched conditions to which they were compelled outside its boundaries.

Sometimes they were transformed from pillagers to soldiers by an offer extended by the Roman authorities; more often they snatched a raid when there was for the moment no good garrison in their neighborhood. Then a Roman force would march against them, and if they were not quick at getting away would cut them to pieces. But with the progress of the central decline the attacks of these small bands on the frontiers became more frequent. Frontier towns came to regard such attacks as a permanent peril and to defend themselves against them. Little groups of raiders would sometimes traverse great districts from end to end, and whether in the form of pirates from the sea or of war bands on land, the ceaseless attempts to enjoy or to loot (but principally to enjoy) the conditions that civilization offered grew more and more persistent.

It must not be imagined, of course, that civilization had not occasionally to suffer then, as it had had to suffer at intervals for a thousand years past, the attacks of really large and organized barbaric armies.[4] Thus in the year 404, driven by the pressure of an Eastern invasion upon their own forests, a vast barbaric host under one Radagasius pushed into Italy. The men bearing arms alone were estimated (in a time well used to soldiery and to such estimates) at 200,000.

But those 200,000 were wiped out. The barbarians were always wiped out when they attempted to come as conquerors. Stilicho (a typical figure, for he was himself of barbarian descent, yet in the regular Roman service) cut to pieces one portion of them, the rest surrendered and were sold off and scattered as slaves.

Immediately afterwards you have a violent quarrel between various soldiers who desire to capture the Imperial power. The story is fragmentary and somewhat confused: now one usurper is blamed, and now another, but the fact common to all is that with the direct object of usurping power a Roman General calls in barbarian bands of pillagers (all sorts of small groups, Franks, Suevians, Vandals) to cross the Rhine into Gaul, *not* as barbarian "conquerors," but as allies, to help in a civil war.

The succeeding generation has left us ample evidence of the results. It presents us with documents that do not give a picture of a ruined province by any means; only of a province which has been traversed in certain directions by the march of barbarian robber bands, who afterwards disappeared, largely in fighting among themselves.

We have, later, the very much more serious business of the Mongol Attila and his Huns, leading the great outer mass of Germans and Slavs into the Empire on an enormous raid. In the middle of the fifth century, fifty years after the destruction of Radagasius, these Asiatics, leading more numerous other barbaric dependents of theirs from the Germanies and the eastern Slavonic lands, penetrated for two brief moments into Northern

---

4. For instance, a century and a half before the breakdown of central Government, the Goths, a barbaric group, largely German, had broken in and ravaged in a worse fashion than their successors in the fifth century.

Italy and Eastern Gaul. The end of that business—infinitely graver though it was than the raids that came before it—is just what one might have expected. The regular and auxiliary disciplined forces of the Empire destroy the barbarian power near Chalons, and the last and worst of the invasions is wiped out as thoroughly as had been all the others.

In general, the barbaric eruptions into the Empire failed wholly as soon as Imperial troops could be brought up to oppose them.

What, then, were the supposed barbaric successes? What was the real nature of the action of Alaric, for instance, and his sack of Rome; and how, later, do we find local "kings" in the place of the Roman Governors?

The real nature of the action of men like Alaric is utterly different from the imaginary picture with which the *old* picturesque popular history recently provided us. That false history gives us the impression of a barbarian Chieftain gathering his Clan to a victorious assault on Rome. Consider the truth upon Alaric and contrast it with this imaginary picture.

Alaric was a young noble of Gothic blood, but from birth a Roman; at eighteen years of age he was put by the Court in command of a small Roman auxiliary force *originally* recruited from the Goths. He was as much a Roman officer, as incapable of thinking of himself in any other terms than those of the Roman Army, as any other one of his colleagues about the throne. He had his commission from the Emperor Theodosius, and when Theodosius marched into Gaul against the usurper Eugenius, he counted Alaric's division as among the most faithful of his Army.

It so happened, moreover, that those few original auxiliaries—mainly Goths by race—were nearly all destroyed in the campaign. Alaric survived. The remnant of his division was recruited, we know not how, but probably from all kinds of sources, to its old strength. It was still called "Gothic," though now of the most mixed origin, and it was still commanded by himself in his character of a Roman General.

Alaric, after this service to the Emperor, was rewarded by

further military dignities in the Roman military hierarchy. He was ambitious of military titles and of important command, as are all soldiers.

Though still under twenty years of age and only a commander of auxiliaries, he asks for the title of *Magister Militum,* with the dignity which accompanied that highest of military posts. The Emperor refuses it. One of the Ministers thereupon begins to plot with Alaric, and suggests to him that he might gather other auxiliary troops under his command, and make things uncomfortable for his superiors. Alaric rebels, marches through the Balkan Peninsula into Thessaly and Greece, and down into the Peloponesus; the regulars march against him (according to some accounts) and beat him back into Albania.

There ends his first adventure. It is exactly like that of a hundred other Roman generals in the past, and so are his further adventures. He remains in Albania at the head of his forces, and makes peace with the Government—still enjoying a regular commission from the Emperor.

He next tries a new adventure to serve his ambition in Italy, but his army is broken to pieces at Pollentia by the armies in Italy—under a general, by the way, as barbaric in mere descent as was Alaric, but, like Alaric, wholly Roman in training and ideas.

The whole thing is a civil war between various branches of the Roman service, and is motived, like all the Roman civil wars for hundreds of years before, by the ambitions of generals.

Alaric does not lose his commission even after his second adventure; he begins to intrigue between the Western and Eastern heads of the Roman Empire. The great invasion under Radagasius interrupts this civil war. That invasion was for Alaric, of course, as for any other Roman officer, an invasion of barbaric enemies. That these enemies should be called by this or that barbaric name is quite indifferent to him. They come from outside the Empire and are therefore, in his eyes, cattle. He helps to destroy them, and destroyed they are—promptly and thoroughly.

When the brief invasion was over, Alaric had the opportunity to renew the civil wars within the Empire, and asked for certain arrears of pay that were due to him. Stilicho, the great rival general (himself, by the way, a Vandal in descent), admitted Alaric's right to arrears of pay, but just at that moment there occurred an obscure palace intrigue which was based, like all the real movements of the time, on differences of religion, not of race. Stilicho, suspected of attempting to restore paganism, is killed. In the general confusion certain of the families of the auxiliaries garrisoned in Italy are massacred by the non-military population. As Alaric is a general in partial rebellion against the Imperial authority, these auxiliaries join him.

The total number of Alaric's men was at this moment very small; they were perhaps 30,000. There was no trace of nationality about them. They were simply a body of discontented soldiers; they had not come from across the frontier; they were not invaders; they were part of the long established and regular garrisons of the Empire; and, for that matter, many garrisons and troops of equally barbaric origin sided with the regular authorities in the quarrel. Alaric marches on Rome with this disaffected Roman Army, claiming that he has been defrauded of his due in salary, and leaning upon the popularity of the dead Stilicho, whose murder he says he will avenge. His thirty thousand claim the barbarian slaves within the city, and certain sums of money which had been the pretext and motive of his rebellion.

As a result of this action the Emperor promises Alaric his regular salary as a general, and a district which he may not only command, but plant with his few followers. Even in the height of his success, Alaric again demands the thing which was nearest his heart, the supreme and entirely Roman title of *Magister Militum*, the highest post in the hierarchy of military advancement. But the Emperor again refuses to give that. Alaric again marches on Rome, a Roman officer followed by a rebellious Roman Army. He forces the Senate to make Attalus nominal Emperor of the West, and Attalus to give him the desired title, his very craving for which is most significant of the Roman character of the whole business. Alaric then quarrels with his puppet, deprives him of the insignia of the Empire, and sends them to

Honorius; quarrels again with Honorius, re-enters Rome and pillages it, marches to Southern Italy, dies, and his small army is dismembered.

There is the story of Alaric as it appears from documents and as it was in reality. There is the truth underlying the false picture with which most educated men were recently provided by the anti-Roman bias of recent history.

Certainly the story of Alaric's discontent with his salary and the terms of his commission, his raiding marches, his plunder of the capital, shows how vastly different was the beginning of the fifth century from the society of three hundred years before. It is symptomatic of the change, and it could only have been possible at a moment when central government was at last breaking down. But it is utterly different in motive and in social character from the vague customary conception of a vast barbarian "invasion," led by a German "war lord" pouring over the Alps and taking Roman society and its capital by storm. It has no relation to such a picture.

If all this be true of the dramatic adventure of Alaric, which has so profoundly affected the imagination of mankind, it is still truer of the other contemporary events which false history might twist into a "conquest" of the Empire by the barbarian.

There was no such conquest. All that happened was an internal transformation of Roman society, in which the chief functions of local government fell to the heads of local auxiliary forces in the Roman Army. As these auxiliary forces were now mainly barbaric, so were the personalities of the new local governors.

I have only dealt with the particular case of Alaric because it is the most familiar, and the most generally distorted: a test, as it were, of my theme.

But what is true of him is true of all other auxiliaries in the Armies—even of the probably Slavonic Vandals. These did frankly loot a province—North Africa—and they (and they alone of the auxiliary troops) did revolt against the Imperial system and defy it for a century: but the Vandals themselves were already, before their adventure, a part of the Imperial forces; they were but a nucleus for a mixed host made up of all the varied elements of rebellion present in the country; and their experiment in separation went down at last forever before the Imperial armies. Meanwhile the North African society on which the rebels lived, and which, with their various recruits—Moors, escaped slaves, criminals—they maladministered and half ruined, was and remained Roman.

In the case of local Italian government the case is quite clear. There was never any question of "invasion" or "conquest."

Odoacer held a regular Roman commission; he was a Roman soldier: Theodoric supplanted him by leave of, and actually under orders from, the Emperor. The last and greatest example, the most permanent, Gaul, tells the same story. The Burgundians are auxiliaries regularly planted after imploring the aid of the Empire and permission to settle. Clovis, the Belgian Fleming, fights no Imperial Army. His forebears were Roman officials: his little band of perhaps 8,000 men was victorious in a small and private civil war which made him Master in the North over other rival generals. He defended the Empire against the Eastern barbaric German tribes. He rejoiced in the titles of Consul and Patrician.

There was no destruction of Roman society, there was no breach of continuity in the main institutions of what was now the Western Christian world; there was no considerable admixture (in these local civil wars) of German, Slav, or outer Celtic blood—no appreciable addition at least to the large amount of such blood which, through the numerous soldiers and much more numerous slaves, had already been incorporated with the population of the Roman world.

But in the course of this transformation in the fifth and sixth centuries local government *did* fall into the hands of those who happened to command the main local forces of the Roman Army, and these were by descent barbarian because the Army had become barbarian in its recruitment.

Why local government gradually succeeded the old centralized Imperial Government, and how, in consequence, there slowly grew up the modern nations, we will next examine.

4

THE BEGINNING OF THE NATIONS

European civilization, which the Catholic Church has made and makes, is by that influence still one. Its unity now (as for three hundred years past) is suffering from the grievous and ugly wound of the Reformation. The earlier wounds have been healed; that modern wound we hope may still be healed—we hope so because the alternative is death. At any rate unity, wounded or unwounded, is still the mark of Christendom.

That unity today falls into national groups. Those of the West in particular are highly differentiated. Gaul (or France as we now call it) is a separate thing. The Iberian or Spanish Peninsula (though divided into five particular, and three main, regions, each with its language, of which one, Portugal, is politically independent of the rest) is another. The old European and Roman district of North Africa is but partially re-occupied by European civilization. Italy has quite recently appeared as another united national group. The Roman province of England has (south of the border) formed one united nation for a longer period than any of the others. To England, Scotland has been added.

How did these modern nations arise in the transformation of the Roman Empire from its old simple pagan condition to one complex Christian civilization? How came there to be also nations exterior to the Empire; old nations like Ireland, new nations like Poland? We must be able to answer this question if we are to understand, not only that European civilization has been continuous (that is, one in time as well as one in spirit and in place), but also if we are to know *why* and *how* that continuity was preserved. For one we are and will be, all Europeans. The moment something threatens our common morals from within, we face it, however tardily. We have forgotten what it is to feel a threat from without: but it may come.

We are already familiar with the old popular and false explanation of the rise of the European nations. This explanation tells us that great numbers of vigorous barbarians entered the Roman Empire, conquered it, established themselves as masters, and parceled out its various provinces.

We have seen that such a picture is fantastic and, when it is accepted, destroys a man's historic sense of Europe.

We have seen that the barbarians who burst through the defense of civilization at various times (from before the beginnings of recorded history; through the pagan period prefacing Our Lord's birth; during the height of the Empire proper, in the third century; again in the fourth and the fifth) never had the power to affect that civilization seriously, and therefore were invariably conquered and easily absorbed. It was in the natural course of things this should be so.

I say "in the natural course of things." Dreadful as the irruption of barbarians into civilized places must always be, even on a small scale, the *conquest* of civilization by barbarians is always and necessarily impossible. Barbarians may have the weight to *destroy* the civilization they enter, and in so doing to destroy themselves with it. But it is inconceivable that they should impose their view and manner upon civilized men. Now to impose one's view and manner, *dare leges* (to give laws), is to conquer.

Moreover, save under the most exceptional conditions, a civilized army with its training, discipline and scientific traditions of war, can always ultimately have the better of a horde. In the case of the Roman Empire the armies of civilization did, as a fact, always have the better of the barbarian hordes. Marius had the better of the barbarians a hundred years before Our Lord was born, though their horde was not broken until it had suffered the loss of 200,000 dead. Five hundred years later the Roman armies had the better of another similar horde of barbarians, the host of Radagasius, in their rush upon Italy; and here again the vast multitude lost some 200,000 killed or sold into slavery. We have seen how the Roman generals, Alaric and the others, destroyed them.

But we have also seen that within the Roman Army itself certain auxiliary troops (which may have preserved to some slight extent traces of their original tribal character, and probably preserved for a generation or so a mixture of Roman speech, camp slang, and the original barbaric tongues) assumed greater and greater importance in the Roman Army towards the end of the imperial period—that is, towards the end of the fourth, and in the beginning of the fifth, centuries (say, 350-450).

We have seen why these auxiliary forces continued to increase in importance within the Roman Army, and we have seen how it was only as Roman soldiers, and as part of the regular forces of civilization, that they had that importance, or that their officers and generals, acting as *Roman* officers and generals, could play the part they did.

The heads of these auxiliary forces were invariably men trained as Romans. They knew of no life save that civilized life which the Empire enjoyed. They regarded themselves as soldiers and politicians of the State *in* which—not *against* which—they warred. They acted wholly within the framework of Roman things. The auxiliaries had no memory or tradition of a barbaric life beyond the Empire, though their stock in some part sprang from it; they had no liking for barbarism, and no living communication with it. The auxiliary soldiers and their generals lived and thought entirely within those imperial boundaries which guarded paved roads, a regular and stately architecture, great and populous cities, the vine, the olive, the Roman law and the bishoprics of the Catholic Church. Outside was a wilderness with which they had nothing to do.

Armed with this knowledge (which puts an end to any fantastic theory of barbarian "conquest"), let us set out to explain that state of affairs which a man born, say, a hundred years after the last of the mere raids into the Empire was destroyed under Radagasius, would have observed in middle age. Sidonius Apollinaris, the famous Bishop of Clermont-Ferrand, lived and wrote his classical work at such a date after Alaric's Roman adventure and Radagasius' defeat that the life of a man would span the distance between them; it was a matter of nearly seventy years between those events and his maturity. A grandson of his would correspond to such a spectator as we are imagining; a grandson of that generation might be born before the year 500. Such a man would have stood towards Radagasius' raid, the last futile irruption of the barbarian, much as men, old today, in England, stand to the Indian Mutiny and the Crimean War, to the second Napoleon in France, to the Civil War in the United States. Had a grandson of Sidonius traveled in Italy, Spain and Gaul in his later years, this is what he would have seen:

In all the great towns Roman life was going on as it had always gone on, so far as externals were concerned. The same Latin speech, now somewhat degraded, the same dress, the same division into a minority of free men, a majority of slaves, and a few very rich masters round whom not only the slaves but the mass of the free men also were grouped as dependents.

In every city, again, he would have found a Bishop of the Catholic Church, a member of that hierarchy which acknowledged its center and headship to be at Rome. Everywhere religion, and especially the settlement of divisions and doubts in religion, would have been the main popular preoccupation. And everywhere *save in Northern Gaul* he would have perceived small groups of men, wealthy, connected with government, often bearing barbaric names, and sometimes (perhaps) still partly acquainted with barbaric tongues. Now these few men were as a rule of a special set in religion. They were called *Arians*; heretics who differed in religion from the mass of their fellow citizens very much as the minority of Protestants in an Irish county today differ from the great mass of their Catholic fellows; and that was a point of capital importance.

The little provincial courts were headed by men who, though Christian (with the Mass, the Sacraments, and all Christian things), were yet out of communion with the bulk of their officials and all their taxpayers. They had inherited that odd position from an accident in the Imperial history. At the moment when their grandfathers had received Baptism the Imperial Court had supported this heresy. They had come, therefore, by family tradition, to regard their separate sect (with its attempt to rationalize the doctrine of the Incarnation) as a "swagger." They thought it an odd title to eminence. And this little vanity had two effects. It cut them off from the mass of their fellow citizens in the Empire. It made their tenure of power uncertain and destined to disappear very soon at the hands of men in sympathy with the great Catholic body—the troops led by the local governors of Northern France.

We shall return to this matter of Arianism. But just let us follow the state of society as our grandson of Sidonius would have seen it at the beginning of the Dark Ages.

The armed forces he might have met upon the roads as he traveled would have been rare; their accoutrements, their discipline, their words of command, were still, though in a degraded form, those of the old Roman Army. There had been no breach in the traditions of that Army or in its corporate life. Many of the bodies he met would still have borne the old imperial insignia.

The money which he handled and with which he paid his bills at the inns, was stamped with the effigy of the reigning Emperor at Byzantium, or one of his predecessors, just as the traveler in a distant British colony today, though that province is virtually independent, will handle coins stamped with the effigies of English Kings. But though the coinage was entirely imperial, he would, upon a passport or a receipt for toll and many another official document he handled, often see side by side with and subordinate to the imperial name, the name of *the chief of the local government.*

This phrase leads me to a feature in the surrounding society which we must not exaggerate, but which made it very different from that united and truly "Imperial" form of government which had covered all civilization two hundred to one hundred years before.

The descendants of those officers who from two hundred to

one hundred years before had only commanded regular or auxiliary forces in the Roman Army, were now seated as almost independent local administrators in the capitals of the Roman provinces.

They still thought of themselves, in 550, say, as mere provincial powers within the one great Empire of Rome. But there was now no positive central power remaining in Rome to control them. The central power was far off in Constantinople. It was universally accepted, but it made no attempt to act.

Let us suppose our traveler to be concerned in some commerce which brought him to the centers of local government throughout the Western Empire. Let him have to visit Paris, Toledo, Ravenna, Arles. He has, let us say, successfully negotiated some business in Spain, which has necessitated his obtaining official documents. He must, that is, come into touch with *officials* and with the actual *Government* in Spain. Two hundred years before he would have seen the officials of, and got his papers from, a government directly dependent upon Rome. The name of the Emperor alone would have appeared on all the papers and his effigy on the seals. Now, in the sixth century, the papers are made out in the old official way and (of course) in Latin, all the public forces are still Roman, all the civilization has still the same unaltered Roman character; has anything changed at all?

Let us see.

To get his papers in the Capital he will be directed to the *"Palatium."* This word does not mean "Palace."

When we say "palace" today we mean the house in which lives the real or nominal ruler of a monarchial state. We talk of Buckingham Palace, St. James' Palace, the Palace in Madrid, and so on.

But the original word *Palatium* had a very different meaning in late Roman society. It signified *the official seat of* Government, and in particular the center from which the writs for Imperial taxation were issued, and to which the proceeds of that taxation were paid. The name was originally taken from the Palatine Hill in Rome, on which the Caesars had their private house. As the mask of private citizenship was gradually thrown off by the Emperors, six hundred to five hundred years before, and as the commanders-in-chief of the Roman Army became more and more true and absolute sovereigns, their house became more and more the official center of the Empire.

The term *"Palatium"* thus became consecrated to a particular use. When the center of Imperial power was transferred to Byzantium the word *"Palatium"* followed it; and at last it was applied to *local centers* as well as to the Imperial city. In the laws of the Empire, then, in its dignities and honors, in the whole of its official life, the *Palatium* means the machine of government, local or imperial. Such a traveler as we have imagined in the middle of the sixth century comes, then, to that Spanish *Palatium* from which, throughout the five centuries of Imperial rule, the Spanish Peninsular had been locally governed. What would he find?

He would find, to begin with, a great staff of clerks and officials, of exactly the same sort as had always inhabited the place, drawing up the same sort of documents as they had drawn up for generations, using certain fixed formulae, and doing everything in the Latin tongue. No local dialect was yet of the least importance. But he would also find that the building was used for acts of authority, and that these acts were performed in the name of a *certain person* (who was no longer the old Roman Governor) *and his Council*. It was this local person's name, rather than the Emperor's, which usually—or at any rate more and more frequently—appeared on the documents.

Let us look closely at this new person seated in authority over Spain, and at his Council: for from such men as he, and from the districts they ruled, the nations of our time and their royal families were to spring.

The first thing that would be noticed on entering the presence of this person who governed Spain, would be that he still had all the insignia and manner of Roman Government.

He sat upon a formal throne as the Emperor's delegate had sat: the provincial delegate of the Emperor. On official occasions he would wear the official Roman garments: the orb and the scepter were already his symbols (we may presume) as they had been those of the Emperor and the Emperor's local subordinates before him. But in two points this central official differed from the old local Governor whom he exactly succeeded, and upon whose machinery of taxation he relied for power.

These two points were: first, that he was surrounded by a very powerful and somewhat jealous body of Great Men; secondly, that he did not habitually give himself an imperial Roman title, but was called *Rex*.

Let us consider these points separately.

As to the first point, the Emperor in Byzantium, and before that in Rome or at Ravenna, worked, as even absolute power must work, through a multitude of men. He was surrounded by high dignitaries, and there devolved from him a whole hierarchy of officials, with the most important of whom he continually consulted. But the Emperor had not been officially and regularly bound in with such a Council. His formulae of administration were personal formulae. Now and then he mentioned his great officials, but he only mentioned them if he chose.

This new local person, who had been very gradually and almost unconsciously substituted for the old Roman Governors, the *Rex,* was, on the contrary, a part of his own Council, and all his formulae of administration mentioned the Council as his coadjutors and assessors in administration. This was necessary above all (a most important point) in anything that regarded the public funds.

It must not be imagined for a moment that the *Rex* issued laws or edicts, or (what was much more common and much more vital) levied taxation under the dominion of, or subject to the consent of, these great men about him. On the contrary, he spoke as absolutely as ever the Imperial Governors had done in the past, and indeed he could not do otherwise because the whole machinery he had inherited presupposed absolute power. But some things were already said to be done "with" these great men: and it is of capital importance that we should note this word "with." The phrases of the official documents from that time run more and more in one of half-a-dozen regular formulae, all of which are based upon this idea of the Council and are in general such words as these: "So and so, *Rex,* ordered and commanded *(with his chief men)* that so and so...should be done."

As to the second point: we note the change of title. The authority of the Palatium is a *Rex;* not a Legate nor a Governor, nor a man sent from the Emperor, nor a man directly and necessarily nominated by him, but a *Rex.* Now what is the meaning of that word *Rex?*

It is usually translated by our word "King." But it does not here mean anything like what our word "King" means when we apply it today—or as we have applied it for many centuries. It does not mean the ruler of a large, independent territory. It means a combination of two things when it is used to name these local rulers in the later Roman Empire. It means 1) The *chieftain* of an auxiliary *group of soldiers* who holds an Imperial commission: and it means 2) That man acting as a local governor.

Centuries and centuries before, indeed a thousand years before, the word *Rex* had meant the chieftain of the little town and petty surrounding district of Rome or of some similar neighboring and small state. It had in the Latin language always retained some such connotation. The word *"Rex"* was often used in Latin literature as we use the word "King" in English: *i.e.,* to describe the head of a state, great or small. But as applied to the local rulers of the fifth century in Western Europe, it was not so used. It meant, as I have said, Chieftain or Chief officer of auxiliaries. A *Rex* was not then, in Spain, or in Gaul, a King in our modern sense of the word: he was only the military head of a particular armed force. He was originally the commander (hereditary or chosen or nominated by the Emperor) of an auxiliary force serving as part of the Roman Army. Later, when these troops—originally recruited perhaps from some one barbaric district—changed by slow degrees into a body half police, half noble, their original name would extend to the whole local army. The "Rex" of, say, Batavian auxiliaries, the commander of the Batavian Corps, would probably be a man of Batavian blood, with hereditary position, and would be called *"Rex Bataviorum."* Afterwards, when the recruiting was mixed, he still kept that title, and later still, when the *Batavii,* as such, had disappeared, his fixed title would remain.

There was no similarity possible between the word *Rex* and the word *Imperator,* any more than there is between the words "Miners' Union" or "Trade Conference" and the word "England." There was, of course, no sort of equality. A Roman General in the early part of the process planning a battle would think of a *Rex* as we think of a Divisionary General. He might say: "I shall put my regulars here in the center. My auxiliaries (Huns or Goths or Franks or what not) I shall put here. Send for their 'Rex' and I will give him his orders."

A *Rex* in this sense was a subject and often an unimportant subject of the *Imperator* or Emperor: the *Imperator* being, as we remember, the Commander-in-Chief of the Roman Army, upon which institution the Roman State or Empire or civilization had depended for so many centuries.

When the Roman Army began to add to itself auxiliary troops (drilled of course after the Roman fashion and forming one body with the Roman forces, but contracted for "in bulk," as it were) the chieftains of these barbaric and often small bodies were called in the official language, *Reges.** Thus Alaric, a Roman officer and nothing more, was the *Rex* of his officially appointed auxiliary force; and since the nucleus of that force had *once* been a small body of Goths, and since Alaric held his position as an officer of that auxiliary force because he had once been, by inheritance, a chieftain of the Goths, the word *Rex* was attached to his Imperial Commission in the Roman Army, and there was added to it the name of that particular barbaric tribe with which his command had originally been connected. He was *Rex* of the Roman auxiliary troops called "Goths." The *"Rex"* in Spain was *"Rex Gotorum,"* not *"Rex Hispaniae'*—that was altogether a later idea. The Rex in Northern France was not *Rex Galliae,* he was *"Rex Francorum."* In each case he was the *Rex*

**Reges=plural of *Rex.—Editor,* 1992.*

of the particular auxiliary troop from which his ancestors—
sometimes generations before—had originally drawn their
Imperial Commission and their right to be officers in the Roman
Army.

Thus you will have the *Rex Francorum,* or King of the Franks,
so styled in the Palatium at Paris, as late as, say, 700 A.D. Not
because any body of "Franks" still survived as a separate
corps—they had been but a couple of regiments or so[5] two hundred years before and had long disappeared—but because the
original title had derived from a Roman auxiliary force of
Franks.

In other words, the old Roman local legislative and taxing
power, the reality of which lay in the old surviving Roman
machinery of a hierarchy of officials with their titles, writs, etc.,
was vested in the hands of a man called *"Rex,"* that is, "Commander" of such and such an auxiliary force; Commander of
the Franks, for instance, or Commander of the Goths. He still
commanded in the year 550 a not very large military force on
which local government depended, and in this little army the
barbarians were still probably predominant because, as we have
seen, towards the end of the Empire the stuff of the army had
become barbaric and the armed force was mainly of barbaric
recruitment. But that small military force was also, and as certainly, very mixed indeed; many a slave or broken Roman freed-
man would enlist, for it had privileges and advantages of great
value;[6] no one cared in the least whether the members of the
armed forces which sustained society were Roman, Gallic, Italian, or German in racial origin. They were of all races and origins. Very shortly after—by, say, 600, at latest—the Army had
become a universal rough levy of all sorts and kinds, and the

---

5. We have documentary record. The greater part of the Frankish auxiliaries
under Clovis were baptized with their General. They came to 4,000 men.
6. Hence the "leges" or codes specially regulating the status of these Roman
troops and called in documents the laws of the "Goths" or "Burgundians,"
as the case may be. There is a trace of old barbaric customs in some of
these, sometimes of an exclusive rule of marriage; but the mass of them
are obviously Roman privileges.

restriction of race was forgotten save in a few customs still cling-
ing by hereditary right to certain families and called their "laws."

Again, there was no conception of rebellion against the
Empire in the mind of a *Rex*. All these *Reges* without exception
held their military office and power originally by a commission
from the Empire. All of them derived their authority from men
who had been regularly established as Imperial functionaries.
When the central power of the Emperor had, as a fact, broken
down, the *Rex* as a fact administered the whole machinery without control.

But no *Rex* ever tried to emancipate himself from the Empire
or warred for independence against the Emperor. The *Rex,* the
local man, undertook all government simply because the old
Government above him, the central Government, had failed. No
Rex ever called himself a local *Imperator* or dreamed of calling
himself so; and that is the most significant thing in all the transition between the full civilization of the old Empire and the Dark
Ages. The original Roman armies invading Gaul, Spain, the
western Germanies and Hungary, fought to conquer, to absorb,
to be masters of and makers of the land they seized. No local
governor of the later transition, no *Rex* of Vandal, Goth, Hun,
Frank or Berber or Moor troop ever dreamt of such a thing.
He might fight another local *Rex* to get part of his taxing-power
or his treasure. He might take part in the great religious quarrels
(as in Africa) and act tyrannically against a dissident majority,
but to fight against the *Empire* as such or to attempt *conquest*
and *rule* over a "subject population" would have meant nothing
to him; in theory the Empire was still under one control.

There, then, you have the picture of what held the levers of
the machine of government during the period of its degradation
and transformation, which followed the breakdown of central
authority. Clovis, in the north of France, the Burgundian chieftain
at Arles, Theodoric in Italy, Athanagild later at Toledo in Spain,
were all of them men who had stepped into the shoes of an
unbroken local Roman administration, who worked entirely by
it, and whose machinery of administration wherever they went
was called by the Roman and official name of *Palatium*.

Their families were originally of barbaric stock: they had for their small armed forces a military institution descended and derived from the Roman auxiliary forces; often, especially in the early years of their power, they spoke a mixed and partly barbaric tongue[7] more easily than pure Latin; but every one of them was a soldier of the declining Empire and regarded himself as a part of it, not as even conceivably an enemy of it.

When we appreciate this we can understand how insignificant were those changes of frontier which make so great a show in historical atlases.

The *Rex* of such and such an auxiliary force dies and divides his "kingdom" between two sons. What does that mean? Not that a nation with its customs and its whole form of administration was suddenly divided into two, still less that there has been what today we call "annexation" or "partition" of states. It simply means that the honor and advantage of administration are divided between the two heirs, who take, the one the one area, the other the other, over which to gather taxes and to receive personal profit. It must always be remembered that the personal privilege so received was very small in comparison with the total revenue to be administrated, and that the vast mass of public work as carried on by the judiciary, the officers of the Treasury and so forth, continued to be quite impersonal and fundamentally imperial. This governmental world of clerks and civil servants lived its own life and was only in theory dependent upon the *Rex*, and the *Rex* was no more than the successor of the chief local Roman official.[8]

The *Rex*, by the way, called himself always by some definite inferior Roman title, such as *Vir Illuster,* as an Englishman today

---

7. The barbaric dialects outside the Empire were already largely latinized through commerce with the Empire and by its influence, and, of course, what we call "Teutonic Languages" are in reality half Roman, long before we get our first full documents in the eighth and ninth centuries.

8. Our popular historical atlases render a very bad service to education by their way of coloring these districts as though they were separate modern nations. The real division right up to full tide of feudalism was Christian and Pagan, and, within the former, Eastern and Western: Greek and Latin.

might be called "Sir Charles So and So" or "Lord So and So," never anything more; and often (as in the case of Clovis), he not only accepted directly from the Roman Emperor a particular office, but observed the old popular Roman customs, such as largesse and procession, upon his induction into that office.

Now why did not this man, this *Rex*, in Italy or Gaul or Spain, simply remain in the position of local Roman Governor? One would imagine, if one did not know more about that society, that he should have done this.

The small auxiliary forces of which he had been chieftain rapidly merged into the body of the Empire, as had the infinitely larger mass of slaves and colonists, equally barbarian in origin, for century after century before that time. The body of civilization was one, and we wonder, at first, why its moral unity did not continue to be represented by a central Monarch. Though the civilization continued to decline, its forms should, one would think, have remained unchanged and the theoretic attachment of each of these subordinates to the Roman Emperor at Constantinople should have endured indefinitely. As a fact, the memory of the old central authority of the Emperor was gradually forgotten; the *Rex* and his local government, as he got weaker, also got more isolated. He came to coining his own money, to treating directly as a completely independent ruler. At last the idea of "kings" and "kingdoms" took shape in men's minds. Why?

The reason that the nature of authority very slowly changed, that the last links with the Roman Empire of the East—that is, with the supreme head at Constantinople—gradually dissolved in the West, and that the modern *nation arose* around these local governments of the *Reges*, is to be found in that novel feature, the standing Council of great men around the *Rex,* with whom everything is done.

This standing Council expresses three forces, which between them were transforming society. Those three forces were: first, certain vague underlying national feelings, older than the Empire, Gallic, Brittanic, Iberian; secondly, the economic force of the great Roman landowners; and, lastly, the living organization of the Catholic Church.

On the economic, or material, side of society, the great land-owners were the reality of that time.

We have no statistics to go upon. But the facts of the time and the nature of its institutions are quite as cogent as detailed statistics. In Spain, in Gaul, in Italy, as in Africa, economic power had concentrated into the hands of exceedingly few men. A few hundred men and women, a few dozen corporations (especially the episcopal sees) had come to own most of the land on which these millions and millions lived; and, with the land, most of the implements and of the slaves.

As to the descent of these great landowners none asked or cared. By the middle of the sixth century only a minority perhaps were still of unmixed blood, but quite certainly none were purely barbaric. Lands wasted or confiscated through the decline of population or the effect of the interminable wars and the plagues lay in the power of the *Palatium,* which granted them out again (strictly under the eye of the Council of Great Men) to new holders.

The few who had come in as original followers and dependents of the "chieftain" of the auxiliary forces benefitted largely; but the thing that really concerns the story of civilization is not the origin of these immensely rich owners (which was mixed), nor their sense of race (which simply did not exist), but the fact that they were so few. It explains both what happened and what was to happen.

That a handful of men, for they were no more than a handful, should thus be in control of the economic destinies of mankind—the result of centuries of Roman development in that direction—is the key to all the material decline of the Empire. It should furnish us, if we were wise, with an object lesson for our own politics today.

The decline of the Imperial power was mainly due to this extraordinary concentration of economic power in the hands of a few. It was these few great Roman landowners who in every local government endowed each of the new administrators, each new Rex, with a tradition of Imperial power, not a little of the dread that went with the old imperial name, and the armed force which it connoted: everywhere the *Rex* had to reckon with the strength of highly concentrated wealth. This was the first element in that standing "Council of Great Men" which was the mark of the time in every locality and wore down the old official, imperial, absolute, local power.

There was, however, as I have said, another and a much more important element in the Council of Great Men, besides the chief landowners; it consisted of the Hierarchy of the Catholic Church.

Every Roman city of that time had a principal personage in it, who knew its life better than anybody else, who had, more than anyone else, power over its morals and ideas, and who in many cases actually administered its affairs. That person was the Bishop.

Throughout Western Europe at that moment men's interest and preoccupation was not race nor even material prosperity, but religion. The great duel between Paganism and the Catholic Church was now decided, after two hard centuries of struggle, in favor of the latter. The Catholic Church, from a small but definite and very tenacious organization within the Empire, and on the whole antagonistic to it, had risen, *first,* to be the only group of men which knew its own mind (200 A.D.); *next,* to be the official religion (300 A.D.); *finally,* to be the cohesive political principle of the great majority of human beings (400 A.D.).

The modern man can distinctly appreciate the phenomenon, if for "creed" he will read "capital," and for the "Faith," "industrial civilization." For just as today men principally care for great fortunes, and in pursuit of them go indifferently from country to country, and sink, as unimportant compared with such an object, the other businesses of our time, so the men of the fifth and sixth centuries were intent upon the *unity* and *exactitude* of religion. That the religion to which the Empire was now converted, the religion of the Catholic Church, should triumph, was their one preoccupation. For *this* they exiled themselves; for *this* they would and did run great risks; as minor to *this* they sank all other things.

The Catholic hierarchy with its enormous power at that moment, civil and economic as well as religious, was not the creator of such a spirit, it was only its leader. And in connection with that intense preoccupation of men's minds, two factors already appear in the fourth century and are increasingly active through the fifth and sixth. The first is the desire that the living Church should be as free as possible; hence the Catholic Church and its ministers everywhere welcome the growth of local as against centralized power. They do so unconsciously but nonetheless strongly. The second factor is Arianism: to which I now return.

Arianism, which both in its material success and in the length of its duration, as well as in its concept of religion and the character of its demise, is singularly parallel to the Protestant movement of recent centuries, had sprung up as the official and fashionable Court heresy opposed to the orthodoxy of the Church.

The Emperor's Court did indeed at last—after many variations—abandon it, but a tradition survived till long after (and in many places) that Arianism stood for the "wealthy" and "respectable" in life.

Moreover, of those barbarians who had taken service as auxiliaries in the Roman armies, the greater part (the "Goths," for instance, as the generic term went, though that term had no longer any national meaning) had received their baptism into civilized Europe from Arian sources, and this in the old time of the fourth century when Arianism was "the thing." Just as we see in eighteenth century Ireland settlers and immigrants accepting Protestantism are "gentlemanly" or "progressive" (some there are so provincial as still to feel thus), so the *Rex* in Spain and the *Rex* in Italy had a family tradition; they, and the descendants of their original companions, were of what had been the "court" and "upper class" way of thinking. They were "Arians" and proud of it. The number of these powerful heretics in the little local courts was small, but their irritant effect was great.

It was the one great quarrel and problem of the time.

No one troubled about race, but everybody was at white heat upon the final form of the Church.

The populace felt it in their bones that if Arianism conquered, Europe was lost: for Arianism lacked vision. It was essentially a hesitation to accept the Incarnation and therefore it would have bred sooner or later a denial of the Sacrament, and at length it would have relapsed, as Protestantism has, into nothingness. Such a decline of imagination and of will would have been fatal to a society materially decadent. Had Arianism triumphed, the aged Society of Europe would have perished.

Now it so happened that of these local administrators or governors who were rapidly becoming independent, and who were surrounded by a powerful court, *one* only was not Arian.

That one was the *Rex Francorum* or chieftain of the little barbaric auxiliary force of "Franks" which had been drawn into the Roman system from Belgium and the banks of the lower Rhine. This body at the time when the transformation took place between the old Imperial system and the beginnings of the nations, had its headquarters in the Roman town of Tournai.

A lad whose Roman name was Clodovicus, and whom his parents probably called by some such sound as Clodovig (they had no written language), succeeded his father, a Roman officer,[9] in the generalship of this small body of troops at the end of the fifth century. Unlike the other auxiliary generals, he was pagan. When with other forces of the Roman Army, he had repelled one of the last of the barbaric invaders close to the frontier at the Roman town of Tolbiacum, and succeeded to the power of local administration in Northern Gaul, he could not but assimilate himself with the civilization wherein he was mixed, and he and most of his small command were baptized. He had already married a Christian wife, the daughter of the Burgundian *Rex;* but in any case such a conclusion was inevitable.

The important historical point is not that he was baptized; for an auxiliary general to be baptized was, by the end of the fifth

---

9. He was presumably head of auxiliaries. His tomb has been found. It is wholly Roman.

century, as much a matter of course as for an Oriental trader from Bombay, who has become an English Lord or Baronet in London in our time, to wear trousers and a coat. The important thing is that he was received and baptized by *Catholics* and not by *Arians*—in the midst of that enormous struggle.

Clodovicus—known in history as Clovis—came from a remote corner of civilization. His men were untouched by the worldly attraction of Arianism; they had no tradition that it was "the thing" or "smart" to adopt the old court heresy which was offensive to the poorer mass of Europeans. When, therefore, this *Rex Francorum* was settled in Paris—about the year 500—and was beginning to administer local government in Northern Gaul, the weight of his influence was thrown with the popular feeling and against the Arian *Reges* in Italy and Spain.

The new armed forces of the *Rex Francorum,* a general levy continuing the old Roman tradition, settling things once and for all by battle, carried orthodox Catholic administration all over Gaul. They turned the Arian *Rex* out of Toulouse, they occupied the valley of the Rhone. For a moment it seemed as though they would support the Catholic populace against the Arian officials in Italy itself.

At any rate, their championship of popular and general religion against the irritant, small, administrative Arian bodies in the *Palatium* of this region and of that, was a very strong lever which the people and the Bishops at their head could not but use in favor of the *Rex Francorum's* independent power. It was, therefore, indirectly, a very strong lever for breaking up the now (500-600) decayed and almost forgotten administrative unity of the Roman world.

Under such forces—the power of the Bishop in each town and district, the growing independence of the few and immensely rich great landowners, the occupation of the *Palatium* and its official machinery by the chieftains of the old auxiliary forces— Western Europe, slowly, very slowly, shifted its political base.

For three generations the mints continued to strike money under the effigy of the Emperor. The new local rulers never took, or dreamed of taking, the Imperial title; the roads were still kept up, the Roman tradition in the arts of life, though coarsened, was never lost. In cooking, dress, architecture, law, and the rest, all the world was Roman. But the visible unity of the Western or Latin Empire not only lacked a civilian and military center, but gradually lost all need for such a center.

Towards the year 600, though our civilization was still one, as it had always been, from the British Channel to the Desert of Sahara, and even (through missionaries) extended its effect a few miles eastward of the old Roman frontier beyond the Rhine, men no longer thought of that civilization as a highly defined area within which they could always find the civilian authority of one organ. Men no longer spoke of our Europe as the *Respublica* or "common weal." It was already beginning to become a mass of small and often overlapping divisions. The things that are older than, and lie beneath, all exact political institutions, the popular legends, the popular feelings for locality and countrysides, were rising everywhere; the great landowners were appearing as semi-independent rulers, each on his own estates (though the many estates of one man were often widely separated).

The daily speech of men was already becoming divided into an infinity of jargons.

Some of these dialects were of Latin origin, some, as in the Germanies and Scandinavia, mixed original Teutonic and Latin; some, as in Brittany, were Celtic; some, as in the eastern Pyrenees, Basque; in North Africa, we may presume, the indigenous tongue of the Berbers resumed its sway; Punic also may have survived in certain towns and villages there.[10] But men paid no attention to the origin of such diversities. The common unity that survived was expressed in the fixed Latin tongue, the tongue of the Church; and the Church, now everywhere supreme in the decay of Arianism and of paganism alike, was the principle of life throughout all this great area of the West.

So it was in Gaul, and with the little belt annexed to Gaul that had risen in the Germanies to the east of the Rhine; so

---

10. We have evidence that it survived in the fifth century.

with nearly all Italy and Dalmatia, and what today we call Switzerland and a part of what today we call Bavaria and Baden;
so with what today we call Spain and Portugal; and so (after
local adventures of a parallel sort, followed by a reconquest
against Arians by Imperial officers and armies) with North
Africa and with a strip of Andalusia.

But *one* part of *one* province *did* suffer a limited and local—
but sharp—change: on one frontier belt, narrow but long, came
something much more nearly resembling a true barbaric success,
and the results thereof, than anything which the Continent could
show. There was here a real breach of continuity with Roman
things.

This exceptional strip was the eastern coast belt of the province of Britain; and we have next to ask: *"What happened in
Britain when the rest of the Empire was being transformed, after
the breakdown of central Imperial power?"* Unless we can
answer that question we shall fail to possess a true picture of
the continuity of Europe and of the early perils in spite of which
that continuity has survived.

I turn, therefore, next to answer the question: "What happened
in Britain?"

5

WHAT HAPPENED IN BRITAIN?

I have now carried this study through four sections. My object in writing it is to show that the Roman Empire never perished but was only transformed; that the Catholic Church, which, in its maturity, it accepted, caused it to survive and was, in that origin of Europe, and has since remained, the soul of one Western civilization.

In the first chapter I sketched the nature of the Roman Empire, in the second the nature of the Church within the Roman Empire before that civilization in its maturity accepted the Faith. In the third I attempted to lay before the reader that transformation and material decline (it was also a *survival*) which has erroneously been called "the fall" of the Roman Empire. In the fourth I presented a picture of what society must have seemed to an onlooker just after the crisis of that transformation and at the entry into what are called the Dark Ages: the beginnings of the modern European nations which have superficially differentiated from the old unity of Rome.

I could wish that space had permitted me to describe a hundred other contemporary things which would enable the reader to seize both the magnitude and the significance of the great change from Pagan to Christian times. I should in particular have dwelt upon the transformation of the European mind with its increasing gravity, its ripening contempt for material things, and its resolution upon the ultimate fate of the human soul, which it now had firmly concluded to be personally immortal and subject to a conscious destiny.

This doctrine of *personal* immortality is the prime mark of the European and stamps his leadership upon the world.

Its original seat—long before history begins—lay perhaps in Ireland, later in Britain, certainly reduced to definition either in Britain or in Gaul. It increasingly influenced Greece and even had some influence upon the Jews before the Romans subdued them. But it remained an opinion, an idea looming in the dark, till it was seen strong and concrete in the full light of the Catholic Church. Oddly enough, Mahomet, who in most things reacted towards weakness of flesh and spirit, adopted this Western doctrine fully; it provided his system with its vigor. Everywhere is that doctrine of immortality the note of superior intelligence and will, especially in its contrast with the thin pantheism and negations of Asia. Everywhere does it accompany health and decision.

Its only worthy counterpart (equally European but rare, uprooted and private) is the bold affirmation of complete and final death.

The transformation of the Roman Empire, then, in the fourth century and the fifth, was eventually its preservation, in peril of full decay, by its acceptation of the Faith.

To this I might have attached the continued carelessness for the plastic arts and for much in letters, the continued growth in holiness, and all that "salting," as it were, which preserved civilization and kept it whole until, after the long sequestration of the Dark Ages, it should discover an opportunity for revival.

My space has not permitted me to describe these things, I must turn at once to the last, and what is for my readers the chief, of the historical problems presented by the beginning of the Dark Ages. That problem is the fate of Britain.

The importance of deciding what happened in Britain when the central government of Rome failed does not lie in the fact that an historical conclusion one way or the other can affect the truth. European civilization is still one, whether men see that unity or no. The Catholic Church is still the soul of it, whether men know it or do not know it. But the problem presented by the fate of Britain at that critical moment when the provinces of the Roman Empire became independent of any common secular control, has this practical importance: that those who read it wrongly and who provide their readers with a false solution (as the Protestant German school and their copiers in English, Freeman, Green and the rest have done), those who talk of "the coming of the English," "the Anglo-Saxon conquest," and the rest, not only furnish arguments against the proper unity of our European story but also produce a warped attitude in the mind. Such men as are deceived by false accounts of the fate of Britain at the entry into the Dark Ages, take for granted many other things historically untrue. Their presumptions confuse or conceal much else that is historical truth: for instance, the character of the Normans; and even contemporary and momentous truth before our eyes today: for instance, the gulf between Englishmen and Prussians. They not only render an Englishman ignorant of his own nation and therefore of himself, they also render all men ignorant of Europe: for a knowledge of Britain in the period 500-700 as in the period 1530-1630 is the test of European history: and if you are wrong on these two points you are wrong on the whole.

A man who desires to make out that the Empire—that is, European civilization—was "conquered" by barbarians cannot today, in the light of modern research, prove his case in Gaul, in Italy, in Spain, or in the valley of the Rhine. The old German thesis of a barbaric "conquest" upon the Continent, possible when modern history was a child, has necessarily been abandoned in its maturity. But that thesis still tries to make out a plausible case when it speaks of Britain, because so much of the record here is lost that there is more room for make-believe; and having made it out, the tale of a German and barbaric England, his false result will powerfully affect modern and immediate conclusions upon our common civilization, upon our institutions, and their nature, and in particular upon the Faith and its authority in Europe.

For if *Britain* be something other than *England*: if what we now know is not original to this Island, but is of the Northern German barbarism in race and tradition, if, in the breakdown of the Roman Empire, Britain was the one exceptional province which really did become a separate barbaric thing, cut off at the roots from the rest of civilization, then those who desire to believe that the institutions of Europe are of no universal effect, that the ancient laws of the Empire—as on property and marriage—were local, and in particular that the Reformation was the revolt of a race—and of a strong and conquering race—against the decaying traditions of Rome, have something to stand on. It does not indeed help them to prove that our civilization is bad or that the Faith is untrue, but it permits them to despair of, or to despise, the unity of Europe, and to regard the present Protestant world as something which is destined to supplant that unity.

Such a point of view is wrong historically as it is wrong in morals. It will find no basis of military success in the future any more than it has in the past.[11] It must ultimately break down if ever it should attempt to put into practice its theory of superiority in barbaric things. But meanwhile as a self-confident theory it can do harm indefinitely great by warping a great section of the European mind; bidding it refer its character to imaginary barbaric origins, so divorcing it from the majestic spirit of Western Civilization. The North German "Teutonic" school of false popular history can create its own imaginary past, and lend to such a figment the authority of antiquity and of lineage.

To show how false this modern school of history has been, but also what opportunities it had for advancing its thesis, is the object of what follows.

Britain, be it remembered, is today the only part of the Roman world in which a conscious antagonism to the ancient and permanent civilization of Europe exists. The Northern Germanies and Scandinavia, which have had, since the Reformation, a religious agreement with all that is still politically powerful in Britain, lay outside the old civilization. They would not have survived the schism of the sixteenth century had Britain resisted that schism. When we come to deal with the story of the Refor-

---

11. I wrote and first printed these words in 1912. I leave them standing with greater force in 1920.

mation in Britain, we shall see how the strong popular resistance to the Reformation nearly overcame that small wealthy class which used the religious excitement of an active minority as an engine to obtain material advantage for themselves. But as a fact in *Britain* the popular resistance to the Reformation failed. A violent and almost universal persecution directed, in the main by the wealthier classes, against the religion of the English populace and the wealth which endowed it just happened to succeed. In little more than a hundred years the newly enriched had won the battle. By the year 1600 the Faith of the British masses had been stamped out from the Highlands to the Channel.

It is our business to understand that this phenomenon, the moral severance of Britain from Europe, was a phenomenon of the sixteenth century and not of the fifth, and that Britain was in no way predestined by race or tradition to so lamentable and tragic a loss.

Let us state the factors in the problem.

The main factor in the problem is that the history of Great Britain from just before the middle of the fifth century (say the years 420 to 445) until the landing of St. Augustine [of Canterbury] in 597 is a blank.

It is of the first importance to the student of the general history in Europe to seize this point. It is true of no other Roman western province, and the truth of it has permitted a vast amount of empty assertion, most of it recent, and nearly all of it as demonstrably (as it is obviously) created by a religious bias. When there is no proof or record men can imagine almost anything, and the anti-Catholic historians have stretched imagination to the last possible limit in filling this blank with whatever could tell against the continuity of civilization.

It is the business of those who love historic truth to get rid of such speculations as of so much rubbish, and to restore to the general reader the few certain facts upon which he can solidly build.

Let me repeat that, had Britain remained true to the unity of Europe in that unfortunate oppression of the sixteenth century which ended in the loss of the Faith, had the populace stood firm or been able to succeed in the field and under arms, or to strike terror into their oppressors by an efficient revolt, in other words had the England of the Tudors remained Catholic, the solution of this ancient problem of the early Dark Ages would present no immediate advantage, nor perhaps would the problem interest men even academically. England would now be one with Europe as she had been for a thousand years before the uprooting of the Reformation. But, as things are, the need for correction is immediate and its success of momentous effect. No true historian, even though he should most bitterly resent the effect of Catholicism upon the European mind, can do other than combat what was, until quite recently, the prevalent teaching with regard to the fate of Britain when the central government of the Empire decayed.

I will first deal with the evidence—such as it is—which has come down to us upon the fate of Britain during the fifth and sixth centuries, and next consider the conclusions to which such evidence should lead us.

THE EVIDENCE

When we have to deal with a gap in history (and though none in Western European history is so strangely empty as this, yet there are very many minor ones which enable us to reason from their analogy), two methods of bridging the gap are present to the historian. The first is research into such rare contemporary records as may illustrate the period: the second is the parallel of what has happened elsewhere in the same case, or better still (when that is possible) the example of what was proceeding in similar places and under similar circumstances at the same time. And there is a third thing: both of these methods must be submitted to the criterion of common sense more thoroughly and more absolutely than the evidence of fuller periods. For when you have full evidence, even of a thing extraordinary, you must admit its truth. But when there is little evidence, guesswork comes in, and common sense is the correction of guesswork.

If, for instance, I learn, as I can learn from contemporary records and from the witness of men still living, that at the battle of Gettysburg infantry advanced so boldly as to bayonet gunners at their guns, I must believe it although the event is astonishing.

If I learn, as I can learn, that a highly civilized and informed government like that of the French in 1870, entering into a war against a great rival, had only the old muzzle-loading cannon when their enemies were already equipped with modern breech-loading pieces, I must accept it on overwhelming evidence, in spite of my astonishment.

When even the miraculous appears in a record—if its human evidence is multiple, converging and exact—I must accept it or deny the value of human evidence.

But when I am dealing with a period or an event for which evidence is lacking or deficient, then obviously it is a sound criterion of criticism to accept the probable and not to presuppose the improbable. Common sense and general experience are nowhere more necessary than in their application, whether in a court of law or in the study of history, to those problems whose difficulty consists in the absence of direct proof.[12]

Remembering all this, let us first set down what is positively known from record with regard to the fate of Britain in the hundred and fifty years of "the gap."

We begin by noting that there were many groups of German soldiery in Britain before the Pirate raids and that the southwest was—whether on account of earlier pirate raids or on account of Saxon settlers the descendants of Roman soldiers—called "the Saxon shore" long before the Imperial system broke down.

Next we turn to documents.

There is exactly one contemporary document professing to tell us anything at all of what happened within this considerable period, exactly one document set down by a witness; and that

---

12. For instance, there is no contemporary account mentioning London during the last half of the fifth and nearly all the sixth century. Green, Freeman, Stubbs, say (making it up as they go along) that London ceased to exist: disappeared! Then (they assert) after a long period of complete abandonment it was laboriously cleared by a totally new race of men and as laboriously rebuilt on exactly the same site. The thing is not physically impossible, but it is so exceedingly improbable that common sense laughs at it.

document is almost valueless for our purpose.

It bears the title, *De Excidio Brittaniae Liber Querulus.* St. Gildas, a monk, was its author. The exact date of its compilation is a matter of dispute—necessarily so, for the whole of that time is quite dark. But it is certainly not earlier than 545. So it was written one hundred years after the beginning of that darkness which covers British history for one hundred and fifty years; most of the Roman regulars had been called away for a continental campaign in 410. They had often so left the island before. But this time the troops sent out on expedition did not return. Britain was visited in 429 and 447 by men who left records. It was not till 597 that St. Augustine landed. St. Augustine landed only fifty years at the most after Gildas wrote his *Liber Querulus,* whereas the snapping of the links between the Continent and southeastern Britain had taken place at least a hundred years before.

Well, it so happens that this book is, as I have called it, almost valueless for history. It is good in morals; its author complains, as all just men must do in all times, of the wickedness of powerful men, and of the vices of princes. It is a homily. The motive of it is not history, but the reformation of morals. In all matters extending to more than a lifetime before that of the writer, in all matters, that is, on which he could not obtain personal evidence, he is hopelessly at sea. He is valuable only as giving us the general impression of military and social struggles as they struck a monk who desired to make them the text of a sermon.

He vaguely talks of Saxon auxiliaries from the North Sea being hired (in the traditional Roman manner) by some Prince in Roman Britain to fight savages who had come out of the Highlands of Scotland and were raiding. He says this use of new auxiliaries began after the Third Consulship of Aëtius (whom he calls "Agitius"), that is, after 446 A.D. He talks still more vaguely of the election of local kings to defend the island from the excesses of these auxiliaries. He is quite as much concerned with the incursions of robber bands of Irish and Scotch into the civilized Roman province as he is with the few Saxon auxiliaries who were thus called in to supplement the arms of the Roman provincials.

He speaks only of a handful of these auxiliaries, three boat-loads; but he is so vague and ill-instructed on the whole of this early period—a hundred years before his time—that one must treat his account of the transaction as half legendary. He tells us that "more numerous companies followed," and we know what that means in the case of the Roman auxiliaries throughout the Empire, a few thousand armed men.

He goes on to say that these auxiliaries, mutinying for pay (another parallel to what we should expect from the history of all the previous hundred years all over Europe), threatened to plunder the civil population. Then comes one sentence of rhetoric saying how they ravaged the countrysides "in punish-ment for our previous sins," until the "flames" of the tumult actually "licked the Western Ocean." It is all (and there is much more) just like what we read in the rhetoric of the lettered men on the Continent who watched the comparatively small but destructive bands of barbarian auxiliaries in revolt, with their accompaniment of escaped slaves and local ne'er-do-wells, cross-ing Gaul and pillaging. If we had no record of the continental troubles but that of some one religious man using a local disaster as the opportunity for a moral discourse, historians could have talked of Gaul exactly as they talk of Britain on the sole authority of St. Gildas. All the exaggeration to which we are used in con-tinental records is here: the "gleaming sword" and the "flame crackling," the "destruction" of cities (which afterward quietly continue an unbroken life!) and all the rest of it. We know per-fectly well that on the Continent similar language was used to describe the predatory actions of little bodies of barbarian aux-iliaries; actions calamitous and tragic no doubt, but not universal and in no way finally destructive of civilization.

It must not be forgotten that St. Gildas also tells us of the return home of many barbarians with plunder (which is again what we should have expected). But at the end of this account he makes an interesting point which shows that—even if we had nothing but his written record to judge by—the barbarian pirates had got some sort of foothold on the eastern coasts of the island.

For after describing how the Romano-British of the province

organized themselves under one Ambrosius Aurelianus, and stood their ground, he tells us that "sometimes the citizens" (that is, the Roman and civilized men), "sometimes the enemy were successful," down to the thorough defeat of some raiding body or other of the Pagans at an unknown place which he calls "Mons Badonicus." This decisive action, he also tells us, took place in the year of his own birth.

Now the importance of this last point is that Gildas after that date can talk of things which he really knew. Let anyone who reads this page recall a great event contemporary with or nearly following his own birth, and see how different is his knowledge of it from his knowledge of that which came even a few years before. This is so today with all the advantages of full record. How much greater would be the contrasts between things really known and hearsay when there was none!

This defeat of the pagan Pirates at Mt. Badon Gildas calls the last but not the least slaughter of the barbarians; and though he probably wrote in the West of Britain, yet we know certainly from his contemporary evidence *that during the whole of his own lifetime up to the writing of his book*—a matter of some forty-four years—there was no more serious fighting. In other words, we are *certain* that the little pagan courts settled on the east coast of Britain were balanced by a remaining mass of declining Roman civilization elsewhere, and that there was no attempt at anything like expansion or conquest from the east westward. For this state of affairs, remember, we have direct contemporary evidence during the whole lifetime of a man and up to within at the most fifty years—perhaps less—from the day when St. Augustine landed in Kent and restored record and letters to the east coast.

We have more rhetoric and more homilies about the "deserted cities and the wickedness of men and the evil life of the Kings"; but that you might hear at any period. All we really get from Gildas is: 1) the confused tradition of a rather heavy predatory raid conducted by barbaric auxiliaries summoned from across the North Sea in true Roman fashion to help a Roman province against uncivilized invaders, Scotch and Irish; 2) (which is most important) the obtaining by these auxiliary troops or their rulers (though in small numbers, it is true) of political power over some territory within the island; 3) the early cessation of any racial struggle, or conflict between Christian and Pagan, or between Barbarian and Roman, even of so much as would strike a man living within the small area of Britain, and the confinement of the new little pagan Pirate courts to the east coast during the whole of the first half of the sixth century.

Here let us turn the light of common sense on to these most imperfect, confused and few facts which Gildas gives us. What sort of thing would a middle-aged man, writing in the decline of letters and with nothing but poor and demonstrably distorted verbal records to go by, set down with regard to a piece of warfare, if a) that man were a monk and a man of peace, b) his object were obviously not history, but a sermon on morals, and c) the fighting was between the Catholic Faith, which was all in all to the men of his time, and Pagans? Obviously he would make all he could of the old and terrified legends of the time long before his birth, he would get more precise as his birth approached (though always gloomy and exaggerating the evil), and he would begin to tell us precise facts with regard to the time he could himself remember. Well, all we get from St. Gildas is the predatory incursions of pagan savages from Scotland and Ireland, long, long before he was born; a small number of auxiliaries called in to help the Roman Provincials against these; the permanent settlement of these auxiliaries in some quarter or other of the island (we know from other evidence that it was the east and southeast coast); and d) what is of capital importance because it is really contemporary, *the settling down of the whole matter, apparently during Gildas' own lifetime in the sixth century*—from say 500 A.D. or earlier to say 545 or later.

I have devoted so much space to this one writer, whose record would hardly count in a time where any sufficient historical document existed, because his book is *absolutely the only one contemporary piece of evidence we have upon the pirate, or*

Saxon, raiding of Britain.[13] There are interesting fragments about it in the various documents known (to us) collectively today as "The Anglo-Saxon Chronicle"—but these documents were compiled many hundreds of years afterwards and had nothing better to go on than St. Gildas himself and possibly a few vague legends.

Now we happen to have in this connection a document which, though not contemporary must be considered as evidence of a kind. It is sober and full, written by one of the really great men of Catholic and European civilization, written in a spirit of wide judgment and written by a founder of history, the Venerable Bede.

True, the Venerable Bede's *Ecclesiastical History* was not produced until *three hundred years after* the first raids of these predatory bands, not until nearly two hundred years after St. Gildas, and not until one hundred and forty years after reading and writing and the full tide of Roman civilization had come back to Eastern Britain with St. Augustine: but certain fundamental statements of his are evidence.

Thus the fact that the Venerable Bede takes for granted permanent pirate settlements (established as regular, if small, states), all the way along the North Sea coast from the northern part of Britain in which he wrote, brought down to the central south by Southampton Water, is a powerful or rather a conclusive argument in favor of the existence of such states some time before he wrote. It is not credible that a man of this weight would write as he does without solid tradition behind him; and he tells us that the settlers on this coast of Britain came from three lowland Frisian tribes, German and Danish, called Saxons, Jutes and Angles.

The first name "Saxon" was *at that time* the name of certain pirates inhabiting two or three small islands on the coasts

---

13. The single sentence in Prosper is insignificant—and what is more, demonstrably false as it stands.

between the Elbe and the Rhone.[14] Ptolemy puts these "Saxons" two hundred years earlier, just beyond the mouth of the Elbe; the Romans knew them as scattered pirates in the North Sea, irritating the coasts of Gaul and Britain for generations. The name later spread to a large island confederation: but that was the way with German tribal names. The German tribal names do not stand for fixed races or even provinces, but for chance agglomerations which suddenly rise and as suddenly disappear. The local term, "Saxon," in the fifth and sixth century had nothing to do with the general term, "Saxon," applied to all northwest of the Germanies two hundred years and more afterwards. These pirates then provided small bands of fighting men under chieftains who founded small organized governments north of the Thames Estuary, at the head of Southampton Water, and on the Sussex coast, when they may or may not have found (but more probably *did* find) existing settlements of their own people already established as colonies by the Romans. The chiefs very probably captured the Roman fiscal organization of the place, but seem rapidly to have degraded society by their barbaric incompetence. They learnt no new language, but continued to talk that of their original seat on the Continent, which language was split up into a number of local dialects, each of which was a mixture of original German and adopted Greek, Latin and even Celtic words.

Of the Jutes we know nothing; there is a mass of modern guesswork about them, valueless like all such stuff. We must presume that they were an insignificant little tribe who sent out a few mercenaries for hire; but they had the advantage of sending out the first, for the handful of mercenaries whom the Roman British called into Kent were by all tradition Jutish. The Venerable Bede also bears witness to an isolated Jutish settlement in the Meon Valley near Southampton Water, comparable to the little German

---

14. The name has retained a vague significance for centuries and is now attached to a population largely Slavonic and wholly Protestant, south of Berlin—hundred of miles from its original seat.

colonies established by the Romans at Bayeux in Normandy and near Rennes.

The Angles were something more definite; they held that corner of land where the neck of Denmark joins the mainland of Germany. This we know for certain. There was a considerable immigration of them; enough to make their departure noticeable in the sparsely populated heaths of their district, and to make Bede record the traveler's tale that their barren country still looked "depopulated." How many boatloads of them, however, may have come, we have of course no sort of record: we only know from our common sense that the number must have been insignificant compared with the total free and slave population of a rich Roman province. Their chiefs got a hold of the land far above the Thames Estuary, in scattered spots all up the east coast of Britain, as far as the Firth of Forth.

There are no other authorities. There is no other evidence save St. Gildas, a contemporary and—two hundred years after him, *three* hundred after the first event—Bede. A mass of legend and worse nonsense called the *Historia Brittonum* exists indeed for those who consult it—but it has no relation to historical science nor any claim to rank as evidence. As we have it, it is centuries late, and it need not concern serious history. Even for the existence of Arthur—to which it is the principal witness—popular legend is a much better guide. As to the original dates of the various statements in the *Historia Brittonum,* those dates are guesswork. The legendary narrative as a whole, though very ancient in its roots, dates only from a period subsequent to Charlemagne, much more than a century later than Bede and a time far less cultured.

The life of St. Germanus, who came and preached in Britain after the Roman legions had left, is contemporary, and deals with events sixty years before St. Gildas' birth. It would be valuable if it told us anything about the Pirate settlements on the coast— whether these were but the confirmation of older Roman Saxon garrisons or Roman agricultural colonies or what—but it tells us nothing about them. We know that St. Germanus dealt in a military capacity with "Picts and Scots"—an ordinary barbarian trouble—but we have no hint at Saxon settlements. St. Germanus was last in Britain in 447, and it is good negative evidence that we hear nothing during that visit of any real trouble from the Saxon pirates who at that very time might be imagined, if legend were to be trusted, to be establishing their power in Kent.

That ends the list of witnesses; that is all our *evidence*.[15] To sum up. So far as recorded history is concerned, all we know is this: that probably some, but certainly only few, of the Roman regular forces were to be found garrisoned in Britain after the year 410; that in the Roman armies there had long been Saxon and other German auxiliaries, some of whom could naturally provide civilian groups, and that Rome even planted agricultural colonies of auxiliaries permanently within the Empire; that the south and east coasts were known as "the Saxon shore" even during Imperial times; that the savages from Scotland and Ireland disturbed the civilized province cruelly; that scattered pirates who had troubled the southern and eastern coasts for two centuries, joined the Scotch and Irish ravaging bands; that some of these were taken in as regular auxiliaries on the old Roman model, somewhere about the middle of the fifth century (the conventional date is 445); that, as happened in many another Roman province, the auxiliaries mutinied for pay and did a good deal of bad looting and ravaging; finally that the ravaging was checked, and that the Pirates were thrown back upon some permanent settlements of theirs established during these disturbances along the easternmost and southernmost coasts. Their numbers must have been very small compared with the original population. No town of any size was destroyed.

Now it is most important in the face of such a paucity of information to seize three points:

First, that the ravaging was not appreciably worse, either in the way it is described or by any other criterion, than the troubles which the Continent suffered at the same time and

---

15. On such a body of evidence—less than a morning's reading—did Green build up for popular sale his romantic *Making of England*.

which (as we know) did not *there* destroy the continuity or unity of civilization.

Secondly, that the sparse raiders, Pagan (as were also some few of those on the Continent) and incapable of civilized effort, obtained, as they did upon the Continent (notably on the left bank of the Rhine), little plots of territory which they held and governed for themselves, and in which after a short period the old Roman order decayed in the incapable hands of the newcomers.

But, thirdly (and upon this all the rest will turn), the *position which these less civilized and pagan small courts happened permanently to hold were positions that cut the link between the Roman province of Britain and the rest of what had been the united Roman Empire.*

This last matter—not numbers, not race—is the capital point in the story of Britain between 447 and 597.

The uncivilized man happened, by a geographical accident, to have cut the communication of the island with its sister provinces of the Empire. He was numerically as insignificant, racially as unproductive and as ill-provided with fruitful or permanent institutions as his brethren on the Rhine or the Danube. But on the Rhine and the Danube the Empire was broad. If a narrow fringe of it was ruined it was no great matter: only a retreat of a few miles. Those sea communications between Britain and Europe were narrow—and the barbarian had been established across them.

The circulation of men, goods and ideas was stopped for one hundred and fifty years because the small pirate settlements (mixed perhaps with barbarian settlements already established by the Empire) had, by the gradual breakdown of the Roman ports, destroyed communication with Europe from Southampton Water right north to beyond the Thames.

It seems certain that even the great town of London, whatever its commercial relations, kept up no official or political business beyond the sea. The pirates had not gone far inland; but, with no intention of conquest (only of loot or continued establishment), they had snapped the bond by which Britain lived.

Such is the direct evidence, and such our first conclusion on it.

But of indirect indications, of reasonable supposition and comparison between what came after the pirate settlements and what had been before, there is much more. By the use of this secondary matter added to the direct evidence one can fully judge both the limits and the nature of the misfortune that overtook Britain after the central Roman government failed and before the Roman missionaries, who restored the province to civilization, had landed.

We may then arrive at a conclusion and know what that Britain was to which the Faith returned with St. Augustine. When we know that, we shall know what Britain continued to be until the catastrophe of the Reformation.

I say that, apart from the direct evidence of St. Gildas and the late but respectable traditions gathered by the Venerable Bede, the use of other and indirect forms of evidence permits us to be certain of one or two main facts, and a method about to be described will enable us to add to these a half-dozen more; the whole may not be sufficient, indeed, to give us a general picture of the time, but it will prevent us from falling into any radical error with regard to the place of Britain in the future unity of Europe when we come to examine that unity as it re-arose in the Middle Ages, partly preserved, partly reconstituted, by the Catholic Church.

The historical method to which I allude and to which I will now introduce the reader may properly be called that of *limitations*.

We may not know what happened between two dates; but if we know pretty well how things stood for some time before the earlier date and for sometime after the later one, then we have two "jumping off places," as it were, from which to build our bridge of speculation and deduction as to what happened in the unexplored gap of time between.

Suppose every record of what happened in the United States between 1862 and 1880 to be wiped out by the destruction of all but one insufficient document, and supposing a fairly full knowledge to survive of the period between the Declaration of Independence and 1862, and a tolerable record to survive of the period between 1880 and the present year. Further, let there be ample traditional memory and legend that a civil war took place, that the struggle was a struggle between North and South, and that its direct and violent financial and political effects were felt for over a decade.

The student hampered by the absence of direct evidence might make many errors in detail and might be led to assert, as probably true, things at which a contemporary would smile. But by analogy with other contemporary countries, by the use of his common sense and his knowledge of human nature, of local climate, of other physical conditions, and of the motives common to all men, he would arrive at a dozen or so general conclusions which would be just. What came after the gap would correct the deductions he had made from his knowledge of what came before it. What came before the gap would help to correct false deductions drawn from what came after it. His knowledge of contemporary life in Europe, let us say, or in western territories which the war did not reach, between 1862 and 1880, would further correct his conclusions.

If he were to confine himself to the most general conclusions he could not be far wrong. He would appreciate the success of the North and how much that success was due to numbers. He would be puzzled perhaps by the different positions of the abolitionist theory before and after the war; but he would know that the slaves were freed in the interval, and he would rightly conclude that their freedom had been a direct historical consequence and contemporary effect of the struggle. He would be equally right in rejecting any theory of the colonization of the Southern States by Northerners; he would note the continuity of certain institutions, the non-continuity of others. In general, if he were to state first what he was sure of, secondly, what he could fairly guess, his brief summary, though very incomplete, would not be *off the rails* of history; he would not be employing such a method to produce historical nonsense as so many of our modern historians have done in their desire to prove the English people

German and barbaric in their origins.

This much being said, let me carefully set down what we know with regard to Britain before and after the bad gap in our records, the unknown one hundred and fifty years between the departure of St. Germanus and the arrival of St. Augustine.

We know that before the bulk of Roman regulars left the country in 410, Britain was an organized Roman province. Therefore, we know that it had regular divisions, with a town as the center of each, many of the towns forming the Sees of the Bishops. We know that official records were kept in Latin and that Latin was the official tongue. We further know that the island at this time had for generations past suffered from incursions of Northern barbarians in great numbers over the Scottish border and from piratical raids of seafarers (some Irish, others Germanic, Dutch and Danish in origin) in much lesser numbers, for the amount of men and provisions conveyable across a wide sea in small boats is highly limited.

Within four years of the end of the sixth century, nearly two hundred years after the cessation of regular Roman government, missionary priests from the Continent, acting on a Roman episcopal commission, land in Britain; from that moment writing returns and our chronicles begin again. What do they tell us?

First, that the whole island is by that time broken up into a number of small and warring districts. Secondly, that these numerous little districts, each under its petty king or prince, fall into two divisions: some of these petty kings and courts are evidently Christian, Celtic-speaking and by all their corporate tradition inherit from the old Roman civilization. The other petty kings and courts speak various "Teutonic" dialects, that is, dialects made up of a jargon of original German words and Latin words mixed. The population of the little settlements under these eastern knights spoke, apparently, for the most part the same dialects as their courts. Thirdly, we find that these courts and their subjects are not only mainly of this speech, but also, in the mass, pagan. There may have been relics of Catholicism among them, but at any rate the tiny courts and petty kinglets were pagan and "Teutonic" in speech. Fourthly, the divisions

between these two kinds of little states were such that the
decayed Christians were, when St. Augustine came, roughly
speaking in the West and center of the island, the Pagans on
the coasts of the South and the East.

All this tallies with the old and distorted legends and traditions, as it does with the direct story of Gildas, and also with
whatever of real history may survive in the careful compilation
of legend and tradition made by the Venerable Bede.

The *first* definite historical truth which we derive from this
use of the method of limitations is of the same sort as that to
which the direct evidence of Gildas leads us. A series of settlements had been effected upon the coasts of the North Sea and
the eastern part of the Channel from, let us say, Dorsetshire or
its neighborhood, right up to the Firth of Forth. They had been
effected by the North Sea pirates and their foothold was good.

Now let us use this method of limitations for matters a little
less obvious, and ask, first, what were the limits between these
two main groups of little confused and warring districts; secondly, how far was either group coherent; thirdly, what had survived in either group of the old order; and, fourthly, what novel
thing had appeared during the darkness of this century-and-a-
half or two centuries?[16]

Taking these four points *seriatine:*

1) Further inland than about a day's march from the sea or
from the estuaries of rivers, we have no proof of the settlement
of the pirates or the formation by them of local governments.
It is impossible to fix the boundaries in such a chaos, but we
know that most of the county of Kent and the seacoast of Sussex,
also all within a raiding distance of Southampton Water, and of
the Hampshire Avon, the maritime part of East Anglia and of
Lincolnshire, so far as we can judge, the East Riding of Yorkshire, Durham, the coastal part at least of Northumberland and

---

16. A century-and-a-half from the very last Roman evidence, the visit of St.
Germanus in 447 to the landing of St. Augustine exactly 150 years later
(597); nearly two centuries from the withdrawal of the expeditionary
Roman Army to the landing of St. Augustine (410-597).

the Lothians, were under numerous pagan kinglets, whose courts talked this mixture of German and Latin words called "Teutonic dialects."

What of the Midlands? The region was a welter, and a welter of which we can tell very little indeed. It formed a sort of march or borderland between the two kinds of courts, those of the king-lets and chieftains who still preserved a tradition of civilization, and those of the kinglets who had lost that tradition. This mixed borderland tended apparently to coalesce (the facts of which we have to judge are very few) under one chief. It was later known not under a Germanic or Celtic name, but under the low Latin name of "Mercia," that is, the "Borderland." To the political aspect of this line of demarcation I will return in a moment.

2) As to the second question: What kind of cohesion was there between the western or the eastern sets of these vague and petty governments? The answer is that the cohesion was of the loosest in either case. Certain fundamental habits differentiated East from West, language, for instance, and much more, religion. Before the coming of St. Augustine, all the western and probably most of the central kinglets were Christians; the kinglets on the eastern coasts Pagan.

There was a tendency in the West apparently to hold together for common interests, but no longer to speak of one head. But note this interesting point. The West that felt some sort of com-mon bond called itself the *Cymry,* and only concerned the moun-tain land. It did not include, it carefully distinguished itself from the Christians of the more fertile Midlands and South and East, which it called *"Laghans."*

Along the east coast there was a sort of tradition of common headship, very nebulous indeed, but existent. Men talked of "chiefs of Britain," *"Bretwaldas,"* a word the first part of which is obviously Roman, the second part of which may be Germanic or Celtic or anything, and which we may guess to indicate a titular headship. But—and this must be especially noted—there was no conscious or visible cohesion among the little courts of the east and southeast coasts; there was no conscious and deliberate continued pagan attack against the Western Christians as such in the end of the sixth century when St. Augustine landed, and no Western Celtic Christian resistance, organized as such, to the chieftains scattered along the eastern coast. Each kinglet fought with each, pagan with pagan, Christian with Christian, Christian and pagan in alliance against pagan and Christian in alliance—and the cross divisions were innumerable. You have petty kings on the eastern coasts with Celtic names; you have Saxon allies in Celtic courts; you have Western Christian kings winning battles on the coasts of the North Sea and Eastern kings winning battles nearly as far west as the Severn, etc., etc. I have said that it is of capital importance to appreciate this point—that the whole thing was a chaos of little independent districts all fighting in a hotch-potch and not a clash of warring races or tongues.

It is difficult for us with our modern experience of great and highly conscious nations to conceive such a state of affairs. When we think of fighting and war, we cannot but think of one considerable conscious *nation* fighting against another similar *nation,* and this modern habit of mind has misled the past upon the nature of Britain at the moment when civilization re-entered the South and East of the island with St. Augustine. Maps are published with guesswork boundaries showing the "frontiers" of the "Anglo-Saxon conquest," at definite dates, and modern historians are fond of talking of the "limits" of that conquest being "extended" to such and such points. There were no "frontiers": there was no "conquest" either way—of East over West or West over East. There were no "extending" limits of Eastern (or of Western) rule. There was no "advance to Chester," no "conquest of the district of Bath." There were battles near Bath and battles near Chester, the loot of a city, a counter raid by the Westerners and all the rest of it. But to talk of a gradual "Anglo-Saxon conquest" is an anachronism.

The men of the time would not have understood such language, for indeed it has no relation to the facts of the time.

The kinglet who could gather his men from a day's march round his court in the lower Thames Valley, fought against the kinglet who could gather his men from a day's march round his stronghold at Canterbury. A Pagan Teutonic-speaking Eastern kinglet would be found allied with a Christian Celtic-speaking Western kinglet and his Christian followers; and the allies would march indifferently against another Christian or another pagan.

There was indeed *later* a westward movement in language and habit which I shall mention; that was the work of the Church. So far as warfare goes there was no movement westward or eastward. Fighting went on continually in all directions, from a hundred separate centers, and if there are reliable traditions of an Eastern Pagan kinglet commanding some mixed host once reaching so far west as to raid the valley of the Wiltshire Avon and another raiding to the Dee, so there are historical records of a Western Christian kinglet reaching and raiding the Eastern settlements right down to the North Sea at Bamborough.

3) Now to the third point: What had survived of the old order in either half of this anarchy? Of Roman government, of Roman order, of true Roman civilization, of that *palatium* of which we spoke in a previous chapter, nothing had anywhere survived. The disappearance of the Roman taxing and judicial machinery is the mark of Britain's great wound. It differentiates the fate of Britain from that of Gaul.

The West of Britain had lost this Roman tradition of government just as much as the East. The "Pict and Scot"[17] and the North Sea pirates, since they could not read or write, or build or make a road or do anything appreciably useful—interrupted civilized life and so starved it. The raids did more to break up the old Roman society than did internal decay. The Western chieftains who retained the Roman Religion had thoroughly lost the Roman organization of society before the year 600. The Roman language, probably only really familiar in the towns, seems to have gone; the Roman method of building had certainly gone. In the West the learned could still write, but they must

---

17. The "Scots"—that is, the Irish—were, of course, of a higher civilization than the other raiders of Britain during this dark time. The Catholic Church reached them early. They had letters and the rest long before Augustine came to Britain.

have done so most sparingly, if we are to judge by the absence of any remains. The Church in some truncated and starved form survived indeed in the West; it was the religion to which an Imperial fragment cut off from all other Roman populations might be expected to cling. Paganism seems to have died out in the West; but the mutilated Catholicism that had taken its place became provincial, ill-instructed, and out of touch with Europe. We may guess, though it is only guesswork, that its chief ailment came from the spiritual fervor, ill-disciplined but vivid, of Brittany and of Ireland.

What had survived in the eastern part of Britain? On the coasts, and up the estuaries of the navigable rivers? Perhaps in patches the original language. It is a question whether Germanic dialects had not been known in eastern Britain long before the departure of the Roman legions. But anyhow, if we suppose the main speech of the East to have been Celtic and Latin before the pirate raids, then that main speech had gone.

So, perhaps altogether, certainly for the most part, had religion. So certainly had the arts—reading and writing and the rest. Over-sea commerce had certainly dwindled, but to what extent we cannot tell. It is not credible that it wholly disappeared; but on the other hand, there is very little trace of connection with southern and eastern Britain in the sparse continental records of this time.

Lastly, and perhaps most important, the old bishoprics had gone.

When St. Gregory sent St. Augustine and his missionaries to refound the old Sees of Britain, his original plan of that refounding had to be wholly changed. He evidently had some old imperial scheme before him, in which he conceived of London, the great city, as the Metropolis and the lesser towns as suffragan to its See. But facts were too strong for him. He had to restore the Church in the coasts that cut off Britain from Europe, and in doing so he had to deal with a ruin. Tradition was lost; and Britain is the only Roman province in which this very great break in the continuity of the bishoprics is to be discovered.

One thing did *not* disappear, and that was the life of the towns.

Of course, a Roman town in the sixth or seventh century was not what it had been in the fourth or fifth; but it is remarkable that in all this wearing away of the old Roman structure, its framework (which was, and is, municipal) remained.

If we cast up the principal towns reappearing when the light of history returns to Britain with St. Augustine's missionaries, we find that all of them are Roman in origin; what is more important, we find that the proportion of *surviving* Roman towns centuries later, when full records exist, is even larger than it is in other provinces of the Empire which we know to have preserved the continuity of civilization. Exeter (perhaps Norwich), Chester, Manchester, Lancaster, Carlisle, York, Canterbury, Lincoln, Rochester, Newcastle, Colchester, Bath, Winchester, Chichester, Gloucester, Cirencester, Leicester, Old Salisbury, Great London itself—these pegs upon which the web of Roman civilization was stretched—stood firm through the confused welter of wars between all these petty chieftains, North Sea Pirate, Welsh and Cumbrian and Pennine highlander, Irish and Scotch.

There was a slow growth of suburbs and some substitution of new suburban sites for old city sites—as at Southampton, Portsmouth, Bristol, Huntingdon, etc. It is what you find all over Europe. But there was no real disturbance of this scheme of towns until the industrial revolution of modern times came to diminish the almost immemorial importance of the Roman cities and to supplant their economic functions by the huge aggregations of the Potteries, the Midlands, South Lancashire, the coal fields and the modern ports.

The student of this main problem in European history, the fate of Britain, must particularly note the phenomenon here described. It is the capital point of proof that Roman Britain, though suffering greviously from the Angle, Saxon, Scotch, and Irish raids, and though cut off for a time from civilization, did survive.

Those who prefer to think of England as a colony of barbarians in which the European life was destroyed, have to suppress many a truth and to conceive many an absurdity in order to support their story; but no absurdity of theirs is *worse* than the fiction they put forward with regard to the story of the English towns.

It was solemnly maintained by the Oxford School and its German masters that these great Roman towns, one after the other, were first utterly destroyed by the Pirates of the North Sea, then left in ruins for generations, and then *reoccupied* through some sudden whim by the newcomers! It needs no historical learning to laugh at such a fancy; but historical learning makes it even more impossible than it is laughable.

Certain rare towns, of course, decayed in the course of centuries: the same is true, for that matter, of Spain and Gaul and Italy. Some few here (as many in Spain, in Gaul and in Italy) may have been actually destroyed in the act of war. There is tradition of something of the sort at Pevensey (the old port of Anderida in Sussex) and for some time a forgery lent the same distinction to Wroxeter under the Wrekin. A great number of towns again (as in every other province of the Empire) naturally diminished with the effect of time. Dorchester on the Thames, for instance, seems to have been quite a large place for centuries after the first troubles with the pirates, though today it is only a village; but it did not decay as the result of war. Sundry small towns became smaller still, some few sank to hamlets as generation after generation of change passed over them: but we find just the same thing in Picardy in the Roussillon, in Lombardy and in Aquitaine. What did *not* happen in Britain was a subversion of the Roman municipal system.

Again, the unwalled settlement outside the walled town often grew at the expense of the municipality within the walls. I have given Huntingdon as an example of this; and there is St. Albans, and Cambridge. But these also have their parallels in every other province of the West. Even in distant Africa you find exactly the same thing. You find it in the northern suburb of Roman Paris itself. That suburb turns into the head of the mediaeval town—yet Paris is perhaps the best example of Roman continuity in all Europe.

The seaports naturally changed in character and often in actual site, especially upon the flat, and therefore changeable, eastern shores—and that is exactly what you find in similar circumstances throughout the tidal waters of the Continent. There is not the shadow or the trace of any widespread destruction of the Roman towns in Britain. On the contrary there is, as much or more than elsewhere in the Empire, the obvious fact of their survival.

The phenomenon is the more remarkable when we consider first that the names of Roman towns given above do not pretend to be a complete list (one may add immediately from memory the southern Dorchester, Dover, Doncaster, etc.), and, secondly, that we have but a most imperfect list remaining of the towns in Roman Britain.

A common method among those who belittle the continuity of our civilization is to deny a Roman origin to any town in which Roman remains do not happen to have been noted as yet by antiquarians. Even under that test we can be certain that Windsor, Lewes, Arundel, Dorking, and twenty others, were seats of Roman habitation, though the remaining records of the first four centuries tell us nothing of them. But in nine cases out of ten the mere absence of catalogued Roman remains proves nothing. The soil of towns is shifted and reshifted continually generation after generation. The antiquary is not stationed at every digging of a foundation, or sinking of a well, or laying of a drain, or paving of a street. His methods are of recent establishment. We have lost centuries of research, and, even with all our modern interest in such matters, the antiquary is not informed once in a hundred times of chance discoveries, unless perhaps they be of coins. When, moreover, we consider that for fifteen hundred years this turning and returning of the soil has been going on within the municipalities, it is ridiculous to affirm that such a place as Oxford, for instance—a town of importance in the later Dark Ages—had no Roman root, simply because the modern antiquary is not yet possessed of any Roman remains recently discovered in it: there may have been no town here before the fifth century: but it is unlikely.

One further point must be noticed before we leave this prime matter: had there been any considerable destruction of the Roman towns in Britain, large and small, we should expect it where the pirate raids fell earliest and most fiercely. We should expect to find the towns near the east and the south coast to have disappeared. The historical truth is quite opposite. The garrison of Anderida indeed and of Anderida alone (Pevensey) was, if we may trust a vague phrase written four hundred years later, massacred in war. But Lincoln, York, Newcastle, Colchester, London, Dover, Canterbury, Rochester, Chichester, Portchester, Winchester, the very principal examples of survival, are all of them either right on the eastern and southern coast or within a day's striking distance of it.

As to decay, the great garrison center of the Second Legion, in the heart of the country which the pirate raiders never reached, has sunk to be little Caerleon-upon-Usk, just as surely as Dorchester on the Thames, far away from the eastern coast, has decayed from a town to a village, and just as surely as Richboro', an island right on the pirate coast itself, has similarly decayed! As with destruction, so with decay, there is no increasing proportion as we go from the west eastward towards the Pirate settlements.

But the point need not be labored. The supposition that the Roman towns disappeared is no longer tenable, and the wonder is how so astonishing an assertion should have lived even for a generation. The Roman towns survived, and, with them, Britain, though maimed.

4) Now for the last question: what novel things had come in to Britain with this breakdown of the central Imperial authority in the fifth and sixth centuries? To answer that is, of course, to answer the chief question of all, and it is the most difficult of all to answer.

I have said that presumably on the South and East the language was new. There were numerous Germanic troops permanently in Britain before the legions disappeared, there was a constant intercourse with Germanic auxiliaries: there were probably colonies, half military, half agricultural. Some have even thought that "Belgic" tribes, whether in Gaul or Britain, spoke Teutonic dialects; but it is safer to believe from the combined evidence of place names and of later traditions, that there was a real change in the common talk of most men within a march of the eastern sea or the estuaries of its rivers.

This change in language, if it occurred (and we must presume it did, though it is not absolutely certain, for there may have been a large amount of mixed German speech among the people before the Roman soldiers departed)—this change of language, I say, is the chief novel matter. The decay of religion means less, for when the pirate raids began, though the Empire was already officially Christian at its heart, the Church had only just taken firm root in the outlying parts.

The institutions which arose in Britain everywhere when the central power of Rome decayed—the meetings of armed men to decide public affairs, money compensation for injuries, the organizing of society by "hundreds," etc., were common to all Europe. Nothing but ignorance can regard them as imported into Britain (or into Ireland or Brittany for that matter) by the Pirates of the North Sea. They are things native to all our European race when it lives simply. A little knowledge of Europe will teach us that there was nothing novel or peculiar in such customs. They appear universally among the Iberians as among the Celts, among the pure Germans beyond the Rhine, the mixed Franks and Batavians upon the delta of that river, and the lowlands of the Scheldt and the Meuse; even among the untouched Roman populations.

Everywhere you get, as the Dark Ages approach and advance, the meetings of armed men in council, the chieftain assisted in his government by such meetings, the weaponed assent or dissent of the great men in conference, the division of the land and people into "hundreds," the fine for murder, and all the rest of it.

Any man who says (and most men of the last generation said it) that among the changes of the two hundred years' gap was the introduction of novel institutions peculiar to the Germans, is speaking in ignorance of the European unity and of that vast landscape of our civilization which every true historian should, however dimly, possess. The same things, talked of in a mixture of Germanic and Latin terms between Poole Harbour and the Bass Rock, were talked of in Celtic terms from the Start to Glasgow; the chroniclers wrote them down in Latin terms alone everywhere from the Sahara to the Grampians and from the Adriatic to the Atlantic. The very Basques, who were so soon to begin the resistance of Christendom against the Mohammedan in Spain, spoke of them in Basque terms. But the actual things—the institutions—for which all these various Latin, Basque, German, and Celtic words stood (the blood-fine, the scale of money—reparation for injury, division of society into "hundreds," the Council advising the Chief, etc.) were much the same throughout the body of Europe. They will always reappear wherever men of our European race are thrown into small, warring communities, avid of combat, jealous of independence, organized under a military aristocracy and reverent of custom.

Everywhere, and particularly in Britain, the Imperial measurements survived—the measurement of land, the units of money and of length and weight were all Roman, and nowhere more than in Eastern Britain during the Dark Ages.

Lastly, let the reader consider the curious point of language. No more striking *simulacrum* of racial unity can be discovered than a common language or set of languages; but it is a *simulacrum*, and a *simulacrum* only. It is neither a proof nor a product of true unity. Language passes from conqueror to conquered, from conquered to conqueror, almost indifferently. Convenience, accident, and many a mysterious force which the historian cannot analyze, propagates it, or checks it. Gaul, thickly populated, organized by but a few garrisons of Roman soldiers and one army corps of occupation, learns to talk Latin universally, almost within living memory of the Roman conquest. Yet two corners of Gaul, the one fertile and rich, the other barren, Amorica and the Basque lands, never accept Latin. Africa, though thoroughly colonized from Italy and penetrated with Italian blood as Gaul never was, retains the Punic speech century after century, to the very ends of Roman rule—seven hundred years after the fall of Carthage: four hundred after the end of the Roman Republic!

Spain, conquered and occupied by the Mohammedan, and settled in very great numbers by a highly civilized Oriental race, talks today a Latin only just touched by Arabic influence. Lombardy, Gallic in blood and with a strong infusion of repeated Germanic invasions (very much larger than ever Britain had!) has lost all trace of Gallic accent, even in language, save in one or two Alpine valleys, and of German speech retains nothing but a few rare and doubtful words. The plain of Hungary and the Carpathian Mountains are a tesselated pavement of languages quite dissimilar, Mongolian, Teutonic, Slav. The Balkan States have, *not* upon their westward or European side, but at their extreme opposite limit, a population which continues the memory of the Empire in its speech; and the vocabulary of the Rumanians is *not the Greek of Byzantium,* which civilized them, but the Latin of Rome!

The most implacable of Mohammedans now under French rule in Algiers speak, and have spoken for centuries, not Arabic in any form, but Berber; and the same speech reappears beyond a wide belt of Arabic in the far desert to the south.

The Irish, a people in permanent contrast to the English, yet talk in the main the English tongue.

The French-Canadians, accepting political unity with Britain, retain their tongue and reject English.

Look where we will, we discover in regard to language something as incalculable as the human will, and as various as human instinct. The deliberate attempt to impose it has nearly always failed. Sometimes it survives as the result of a deliberate policy. Sometimes it is restored as a piece of national protest—Bohemia is an example. Sometimes it "catches on" naturally and runs for hundreds of miles, covering the most varied peoples and even the most varied civilizations with a common veil.

Now the Roman towns were not destroyed, the original population was certainly not destroyed even in the few original settlements of Saxon and Angles in the sea and river shores of the East. Such civilization as the little courts of the Pirate chieftains maintained was degraded Roman or it was nothing. But the so-called "Anglo-Saxon" *language*—the group of half-German[18] dialects which may have taken root before the withdrawal of the Roman legions in the East of Britain, and which at any rate were well rooted there a hundred years after—stood ready for one of two fates. Either it would die out and be replaced by dialects half Celtic, half Latin vocabulary, or it would spread westward. That the Teutonic dialects of the eastern kinglets should spread westward might have seemed impossible. The unlettered barbarian does not teach the lettered civilized man; the pagan does not mold the Christian. It is the other way about. Yet in point of fact that happened. Why?

Before we answer that question let us consider another point. Side by side with the entry of civilization through the Roman missionary priests in Kent, there was going on a missionary effort in the North of the Island of Britain, which effort was Irish. It had various Celtic dialects for its common daily medium, though it was, of course, Roman in ritual at the altar. The Celtic missionaries, had they alone been in the field, would have made us all Celtic-speaking today. But it was the direct mission from Rome that won, and this for the reason that it had behind it the full tide of Europe. Letters, order, law, building, schools, re-entered England through Kent—not through Northumberland where the Irish were preaching.

Even so the spread westward of a letterless and starved set of dialects from the little courts of the eastern coasts (from Canterbury and Bamborough and so forth) would have been impossible but for a tremendous accident.

St. Augustine, after his landing, proposed to the native British bishops that they should help in the conversion of the little pagan kinglets and their courts on the eastern coast. They would not.

---

18. I say "*half*-German" lest the reader should think, by the use of the word "German" or "Teutonic," that the various dialects of this sort (including those of the North Sea Pirates) were something original, uninfluenced by Rome. It must always be remembered that with their original words and roots was mixed an equal mass of superior words learned from the civilized men of the South in the course of the many centuries during which Germans had served the Romans as slaves and in arms and had met their merchants.

They had been cut off from Europe for so long that they had become warped. They refused communion. The peaceful Roman Mission coming just at the moment when the Empire had recovered Italy and was fully restoring itself, was thrown back on the Eastern courts. It used them. It backed *their* tongue, *their* arms, *their* tradition. The terms of Roman things were carefully translated by the priests into the Teutonic dialects of these courts; the advance of civilization under the missionaries, recapturing more and more of the province of Britain, proceeded westward from the courts of the Eastern kinglets. The schools, the official world—all—was now turned by the weight of the Church against a survival of the Celtic tongues and in favor of the Eastern Teutonic ones.

Once civilization had come back by way of the South and East, principally through the natural gate of Kent and through the Straits of Dover which had been blocked so long, this tendency of the Eastern dialects to spread as the language of an organized clerical officialdom and of its courts of law was immediately strengthened. It soon and rapidly swamped all but the western hills. But of colonization, of the advance of a race, there was none. What advanced was the Roman organization once more and, with it, the dialects of the courts it favored.

What we know, then, of Britain when it was recivilized we know through Latin terms or through the half-German dialects which ultimately and much later merge into what we call Anglo-Saxon. An historic King of Sussex bears a Celtic name, but we read of him in the Latin, then in the Teutonic tongues, and his realm, however feeble the proportion of over-sea blood in it, bears an over-sea label for its court—"the South Saxon."

The mythical founder of Wessex bears a Celtic name, Cerdic: but we read of him, if not in Latin, then in Anglo-Saxon. Not a *cantref* but a *hundred* is the term of social organization in England when it is re-civilized; not an *eglywys* but a *church*[19]

---

19. This word "church" is a good example of what we mean by Teutonic dialect. It is straight from the Mediterranean. The native German word

is the name of the building in which the new civilization hears
Mass. The ruler, whatever his blood or the blood of his subjects,
is a *Cynning,* not a *Reg* or a *Prins.* His house and court are
a *hall,*[20] not a *plâs.* We get our whole picture of renovated Britain
(after the Church is restored) colored by this half-German
speech. But the Britain we see thus colored is not barbaric. It
is a Christian Britain of mixed origin, of ancient municipalities
cut off for a time by the Pirate occupation of the South and
East, but now reunited with the one civilization whose root is
in Rome.

This clear historical conclusion sounds so novel today that I
must emphasize and confirm it.

Western Europe in the sixth, seventh, and eighth centuries was
largely indifferent to our modern ideas of race. Of nationality
it knew nothing. It was concerned with the maintenance of the
Catholic Church, especially against the outer Pagan. This filled
the mind. This drove all the mastering energies of the time. The
Church, that is, all the acts of life, but especially record and
common culture, came back into a Britain which had been cut
off. It reopened the gate. It was refused aid by the Christian
whom it relieved. It decided for the courts of the South and
East, taught them organization, and carried their dialects with
it through the Island which it gradually recovered for
civilization.

We are now in a position to sum up our conclusions upon
the matter:

Britain, connected with the rest of civilization by a narrow
and precarious neck of sea-travel over the Straits of Dover, had,
in the last centuries of Roman rule, often furnished great armies
to usurpers or Imperial claimants, sometimes leaving the Island
almost bare of regular troops. But with each return of peace
these armies also had returned and the rule of the central Roman
government over Britain had been fairly continuous until the

---

for a temple—if they had got so far as to have temples (for we know nothing of their religion)—is lost.

20. And "hall" is again a Roman word adopted by the Germans.

beginning of the fifth century. At that moment—in 410 A.D.—
the bulk of the trained soldiers again left upon a foreign adventure. But the central rule of Rome was then breaking down:
these regulars never returned—though many auxiliary troops
may have remained.

At this moment, when every province of the West was subject
to disturbance and to the over-running of barbarian bands, small
but destructive, Britain particularly suffered. Scotch, Irish and
German barbarians looted her on all sides.

These last, the Saxon pirates, brought in as auxiliaries in
the Roman fashion, may already have been settled in places
upon the eastern coast, their various half-German dialects may
have already been common upon those coasts; but at any rate,
after the breakdown of the Roman order, detached communities
under little local chiefs arose. The towns were not destroyed.
Neither the slaves, nor, for that matter, the greater part of the
free population fell. But wealth declined rapidly in the chaos
as it did throughout Western Europe. And side by side with
this ruin came the replacing of the Roman official language
by a welter of Celtic and of half-German dialects in a mass
of little courts. The new official Roman religion—certainly at
the moment of the breakdown the religion of a small
minority—almost or wholly disappeared in the Eastern pirate
settlements. The Roman language similarly disappeared in the
many small principalities of the western part of the island; they
reverted to their original Celtic dialects. There was no boundary
between the hotch-potch of little German-speaking territories
on the East and the little Celtic territories on the West. There
was no more than a vague common feeling of West against
East or East against West; all fought indiscriminately among
themselves.

After a time which could be covered by two long lives, during
which decline had been very rapid, and as noticeable in the
West as in the East throughout the Island, the full influence
of civilization returned, with the landing in 597 of St.
Augustine and his missionaries sent by the Pope.

But the little Pirate courts of the East happened to have set-

tled on coasts which occupied the gateway into the Island; it was thus through them that civilization had been cut off, and it was through them that civilization came back. On this account:

1) The little kingdoms tended to coalesce under the united discipline of the Church.

2) The united British civilization so forming was able to advance gradually *westward* across the island.

3) Though the institutions of Europe were much the same wherever Roman civilization had existed and had declined, though the councils of magnates surrounding the King, the assemblies of armed men, the division of land and people into "hundreds" and the rest of it were common to Europe, *these things were given, over a wider and wider area of Britain, Eastern, half-German names because it was through the courts of the Eastern kinglets that civilization had returned.* The kinglets of the East, as civilization grew, were continually fed from the Continent, strengthened with ideas, institutions, arts, and the discipline of the Church. Thus did they politically become more and more powerful, until the whole island—except the Cornish peninsula, Wales and the Northwestern mountains—was more or less administered by the courts which had their roots in the eastern coasts and rivers, and which spoke dialects cognate to those beyond the North Sea, while the West, cut off from this Latin restoration, decayed in political power and saw its Celtic dialects shrink in area.

By the time that this old Roman province of Britain re-arises as an ordered Christian land in the eighth century, its records are kept not only in Latin but in the Court "Anglo-Saxon" dialects: by far the most important being that of Winchester. Many place names, and the general speech of its inhabitants have followed suit, and this, a superficial but a very vivid change, is the chief outward change in the slow transformation that has been going on in Britain for three hundred years (450-500 to 750-800).

Britain is reconquered for civilization and that easily; it is again an established part of the European unity, with the same sacraments, the same morals, and all those same conceptions of human life as bound Europe together even more firmly than the old central government of Rome had bound it. And within this unity of civilized Christendom England was to remain for eight hundred years.

6

THE DARK AGES

So far we have traced the fortunes of the Roman Empire (that is, of European civilization and of the Catholic Church with which that civilization was identified) from the origins both of the Church and of the Empire, to the turning point of the fifth century. We have seen the character of that turning point.

There was a gradual decline in the power of the central monarchy, an increasing use of auxiliary barbarian troops in the army upon which Roman society was founded, until at last (in the years from 400 to 500 A.D.) authority, though Roman in every detail of its form, gradually ceased to be exercised from Rome or Constantinople, but fell imperceptibly into the hands of a number of local governments. We have seen that the administration of these local governments usually devolved on the chief officers of the auxiliary barbarian troops, who were also, as a rule, their chieftains by some kind of inheritance.

We have seen that there was no considerable infiltration of barbarian blood, no "invasions" in our modern sense of the term (or rather, no successful ones); no blotting out of civilization, still less any introduction of new institutions or ideas drawn from barbarism.

The coast regions of Eastern Britain (the strongest example of all, for there the change was most severe) were reconquered for civilization and for the Faith by the efforts of St. Augustine; Africa was recaptured for the direct rule of the Emperor: so was Italy and the South of Spain. At the end of the seventh century that which was in the future to be called Christendom (and which is nothing more than the Roman Empire continuing, though transformed) is again reunited.

What followed was a whole series of generations in which the forms of civilization were set and crystallized in a few very simple, traditional and easily appreciated types. The whole standard of Europe was lowered to the level of its fundamentals, as it were. The primary arts upon which we depend for our food and drink, and raiment and shelter, survived intact. The secondary arts reposing upon these failed and disappeared almost in proportion to their distance from fundamental necessities of our race. History became no more than a simple chronicle. Letters, in the finer sense, almost ceased. Four hundred years more were to pass before Europe was to reawaken from this sort of sleep into which her spirit had retreated, and the passage from the full civilization of Rome through this period of simple and sometimes barbarous things is properly called the Dark Ages.

It is of great importance for anyone who would comprehend the general story of Europe to grasp the nature of those half-hidden centuries. They may be compared to a lake into which the activities of the old world flowed and stirred and then were still, and from which in good time the activities of the Middle Ages, properly so called, were again to flow.

Again, one may compare the Dark Ages to the leafsoil of a forest. They are formed by the disintegration of an antique florescence. They are the bed from which new florescence shall spring.

It is a curious phenomenon to consider: this hibernation, or sleep: this rest of the stuff of Europe. It leads one to consider the flux and reflux of civilization as something much more comparable to a pulse than to a growth. It makes us remember that *rhythm* which is observed in all forms of energy. It makes us doubt that mere progress from simplicity to complexity which used to be affirmed as the main law of history.

The contemplation of the Dark Ages affords a powerful criticism of that superficial theory of social evolution which is among the intellectual plagues of our own generation. Much more is the story of Europe like the waking and the sleeping of a mature man, than like any indefinite increase in the aptitudes and powers of a growing body.

Though the prime characteristic of the Dark Ages is one of recollection, and though they are chiefly marked by this note of Europe sinking back into herself, very much more must be known of them before we have the truth, even in its most general form.

I will put in the form of a category or list the chief points which we must bear in mind.

In the first place the Dark Ages were a period of intense military action. Christendom was besieged from all around. It was held like a stronghold, and in those centuries of struggle its institutions were molded by military necessities: so that Christendom has ever since had about it the quality of a soldier. There was one unending series of attacks, Pagan and Mohammedan, from the North, from the East and from the South; attacks not comparable to the older raids of external hordes, eager only to enjoy civilization within the Empire, small in number and yet ready to accept the faith and customs of Europe. The barbarian incursions of the fifth and sixth centuries—at the end of the United Roman Empire—had been of this lesser kind. The mighty struggles of the eighth, ninth and especially the tenth centuries—of the Dark Ages—were a very different matter. Had the military institutions of Europe failed in *that* struggle, our civilization would have been wiped out; and indeed at one or two critical points, as in the middle of the eighth against the Mohammedan, and at the end of the ninth century against the northern pirates, all human judgment would have decided that Europe *was* doomed.

In point of fact, as we shall see in a moment, Europe was just barely saved. It was saved by the sword and by the intense Christian ideal which nerved the sword arm. But it was only just barely saved.

The first assault came from Islam.

A new intense and vividly anti-Christian thing arose in a moment, as it were, out of nothing, out of the hot sands to the East and spread like a fire. It consumed all the Levant. It arrived at the doors of the West. This was no mere rush of barbarism.

The Mohammedan world was as cultured as our own in its first expansion. It maintained a higher and an increasing culture while ours declined; and its conquest, where it conquered us, was the conquest of something materially superior for the moment over the remaining arts and traditions of Christian Europe.

Just at the moment when Britain was finally won back to Europe, and when the unity of the West seemed to be recovered (though its life had fallen to so much lower a plane), we lost North Africa; it was swept from end to end in one tidal rush by that new force which aimed fiercely at our destruction. Immediately afterwards the first Mohammedan force crossed the Straits of Gibraltar; and in a few months after its landing the whole of the Spanish Peninsula, that strong Rock as it had seemed of ancient Roman culture, the hard Iberian land, crumbled. Politically, at least, and right up to the Pyrenees, Asia had it in its grip. In the mountain valleys alone, and especially in the tangle of highlands which occupies the northwestern corner of the Spanish square, individual communities of soldiers held out. From these the gradual reconquest of Spain by Christendom was to proceed, but for the moment they were crowded and penned upon the Asturian hills like men fighting against a wall.

Even Gaul was threatened: a Mohammedan host poured up into its very center far beyond Poitiers: halfway to Tours. Luckily it was defeated; but Moslem garrisons continued to hold out in the Southern districts, in the northern fringes of the Pyrenees and along the shore line of the Narbonese and Provence.

Southern Italy was raided and partly occupied. The islands of the Mediterranean fell.

Against this sudden successful spring which had lopped off half of the West, the Dark Ages, and especially the French of the Dark Ages, spent a great part of their military energy. The knights of Northern Spain and the chiefs of the unconquered valleys recruited their forces perpetually from Gaul beyond the Pyrenees; and the northern valley of the Ebro, the high plains of Castile and Leon, were the training ground of European valor for three hundred years. The Basques were the unyielding basis of all the advance.

This Mohammedan swoop was the first and most disastrously successful of the three great assaults.

Next came the Scandinavian pirates.

Their descent was a purely barbaric thing, not numerous but (since pirates can destroy much with small numbers) for centuries unexhausted. They harried all the rivers and coasts of Britain, of Gaul, and of the Netherlands. They appeared in the Southern seas and their efforts seemed indefatigable. Britain especially (where the raiders bore the local name of "Danes") suffered from a ceaseless pillage, and these new enemies had no attraction to the Roman land save loot. They merely destroyed. They refused our religion. Had they succeeded they would not have mingled with us, but would have ended us.

Both in Northern Gaul and in Britain their chieftains acquired something of a foothold, but only after the perilous moment in which their armies were checked; they were tamed and constrained to accept the society they had attacked.

This critical moment when Europe seemed doomed was the last generation of the ninth century. France had been harried up to the gates of Paris. Britain was so raided that its last independent king, Alfred, was in hiding.

Both in Britain and Gaul Christendom triumphed, and in the same generation.

Paris stood a successful siege, and the family which defended it was destined to become the royal family of all France at the inception of the Middle Ages. Alfred of Wessex in the same decade recovered South England. In both provinces of Christendom the situation was saved. The chiefs of the pirates were baptized; and though Northern barbarism remained a material menace for another hundred years, there was no further danger of our destruction.

Finally, less noticed by history, but quite as grievous, and needing a defense as gallant, was the pagan advance over the North German Plain and up the valley of the Danube.

All the frontier of Christendom upon this line from Augsburg and the Lech to the course of the Elbe and the North Sea was but a line of fortresses and continual battlefields. It was but recently organized land. Until the generations before the year 800 there was no civilization beyond the Rhine save the upper Danube partially reclaimed, and a very scanty single extension up the valley of the Lower Main.

But Charlemagne, with vast Gallic armies, broke into the barbaric Germanies right up to the Elbe. He compelled them by arms to accept religion, letters and arts. He extended Europe to these new boundaries and organized them as a sort of rampart in the East: a thing the Roman Empire had not done. The Church was the cement of this new belt of defense—the imperfect population of which were evangelized from Ireland and Britain. It was an experiment, this creation of the Germanies by Western culture, this spiritual colonization of a *March* beyond the limits of the Empire. It did not completely succeed, as the Reformation proves; but it had at least the strength in the century after Charlemagne, its founder, to withstand the Eastern attack upon Christendom.

The attack was not racial. It was Pagan Slav, mixed with much that was left of Pagan German, even Mongol. Its character was the advance of the savage against the civilized man, and it remained a peril two generations longer than the peril which Gaul and Britain had staved off from the North.

This, then, is the first characteristic to be remembered of the Dark Ages: the violence of the physical struggle and the intense physical effort by which Europe was saved.

The second characteristic of the Dark Ages proceeds from this first military one: it may be called Feudalism.

Briefly it was this: the passing of actual government from the hands of the old Roman provincial centers of administration into the hands of each small local society and its lord. On such a basis there was a reconstruction of society from below: these local lords associating themselves under greater men, and these again holding together in great national groups under a national overlord.

In the violence of the struggle through which Christendom passed, town and village, valley and castle, had often to defend itself alone.

The great Roman landed estates, with their masses of dependents and slaves, under a lord or owner, had never disappeared. The descendants of these Roman, Gallic, British *owners* formed the fighting class of the Dark Ages, and in this new function of theirs, perpetually lifted up to be the sole depositories of authority in some small imperiled countryside, they grew to be nearly independent units. For the purposes of cohesion, that family which possessed most estates in a district tended to become the leader of it. Whole provinces were thus formed and grouped, and the vaguer sentiments of a larger unity expressed themselves by the choice of some one family, one of the most powerful in every county, who would be the overlord of all the other lords, great and small.

Side by side with this growth of local independence and of voluntary local groupings went the transformation of the old imperial nominated offices into hereditary and personal things.

A *count*, for instance, was originally a *"comes"* or "companion" of the Emperor. The word dates from long before the breakup of the central authority of Rome. A *count* later was a great official: a local governor and judge—the Vice-Roy of a large district (a French county and English shire). His office was revocable, like other official appointments. He was appointed for a season, first at the Emperor's, later at the local King's discretion, to a particular local government. In the Dark Ages the *count* becomes hereditary. He thinks of his government as a possession which his son should rightly have after him. He bases his right to his government upon the possession of great estates within the area of that government. In a word, he comes to think of himself not as an official at all but as a *feudal overlord,* and all society (and the remaining shadow of central authority itself) agrees with him.

The second note, then, of the Dark Ages is the gradual transition of Christian society from a number of slave-owning, rich, landed proprietors, taxed and administered by a regular government, to a society of fighting *nobles* and their descendants, organized upon a basis of independence and in a hierarchy of lord and overlord, and supported no longer by *slaves* in the *villages*, but by half-free serfs, or *"villeins."*

Later an elaborate theory was constructed in order to rationalize this living and real thing. It was pretended—by a legal fiction—that the central King owned nearly all the land, that the great overlords "held" their land of him, the lesser lords "holding" theirs hereditarily of the overlords, and so forth. This idea of "holding" instead of "owning," though it gave an easy machinery for confiscation in time of rebellion, was legal theory only, and, so far as men's views of property went, a mere form. The reality was what I have described.

The third characteristic of the Dark Ages was the curious fixity of morals, of traditions, of the forms of religion, and of all that makes up social life.

We may presume that all civilization originally sprang from a soil in which custom was equally permanent.

We know that in the great civilizations of the East an enduring fixity of form is normal.

But in the general history of Europe, it has been otherwise. There has been a perpetual flux in the outward form of things, in architecture, in dress, and in the statement of philosophy as well (though not in its fundamentals).

In this mobile surface of European history the Dark Ages form a sort of island of changelessness. There is an absence of any great heresies in the West, and, save in one or two names, an absence of speculation. It was as though men had no time for any other activity but the ceaseless business of arms and of the defense of the West.

Consider the life of Charlemagne, who is the central figure of those centuries. It is spent almost entirely in the saddle. One season finds him upon the Elbe, the next upon the Pyrenees. One Easter he celebrates in Northern Gaul, another in Rome. The whole story is one of perpetual marching, and of blows parrying here, thrusting there, upon all the boundaries of isolated and besieged Christendom. He will attend to learning, but the ideal of learning is repetitive and conservative: its passion is to hold what was, not to create or expand. An anxious and sometimes desperate determination to preserve the memory of a great

but half-forgotten past is the business of his court, which dis-
solves just before the worst of the Pagan assault; as it is the
business of Alfred, who arises a century later, just after the
worst assault has been finally repelled.

Religion during these centuries settled and consolidated, as
it were. An enemy would say that it petrified, a friend that it
was enormously strengthened by pressure. But whatever the metaphor chosen, the truth indicated will be this: that the Catholic
Faith became between the years 600 and 1000 utterly one with
Europe. The last vestiges of the antique and Pagan civilization
of the Mediterranean were absorbed. A habit of certitude and
of fixity, even in the details of thought, was formed in the
European mind.

It is to be noted in this connection that geographically the center of things had somewhat shifted. With the loss of Spain and
of Northern Africa, the Mohammedan raiding of Southern Italy
and the islands, the Mediterranean was no longer a vehicle of
Western civilization, but the frontier of it. Rome itself might
now be regarded as a frontier town. The eruption of the barbarians from the East along the Danube had singularly cut off the
Latin West from Constantinople and from all the high culture
of its Empire. Therefore, the center of that which resisted in
the West, the geographical nucleus of the island of Christendom,
which was besieged all round, was France, and in particular
Northern France. Northern Italy, the Germanies, the Pyrenees
and the upper valley of the Ebro were essentially the marches
of Gaul. Gaul was to preserve all that could be preserved of
the material side of Europe, and also of the European spirit.
And therefore the New World, when it arose, with its Gothic
Architecture, its Parliaments, its Universities, and, in general,
its spring of the Middle Ages, was to be a Gallic thing.

The fourth characteristic of the Dark Ages was a material one,
and was that which would strike our eyes most immediately if
we could transfer ourselves in time, and enjoy a physical impression of that world. This characteristic was derived from what
I have just been saying. It was the material counterpart of the
moral immobility or steadfastness of the time. It was this: that

the external forms of things stood quite unchanged. The semi-circular arch, the short, stout pillar, occasionally (but rarely) the dome: these were everywhere the mark of architecture. There was no change nor any attempt at change. The arts were saved but not increased, and the whole of the work that men did with their hands stood fast in mere tradition. No new town arises. If one is mentioned (Oxford, for instance) for the first time in the Dark Ages, whether in Britain or in Gaul, one may fairly presume a Roman origin for it, even though there be no actual mention of it handed down from Roman times.

No new roads were laid. The old Roman military system of highways was kept up and repaired, though kept up and repaired with a declining vigor. The wheel of European life had settled to one slow rate of turning.

Not only were all these forms enduring, they were also few and simple. One type of public building and of church, one type of writing, everywhere recognizable, one type of agriculture, with very few products to differentiate it, alone remained.

The fifth characteristic of the Dark Ages is one apparently, but only apparently, contradictory of that immobile and fundamental character which I have just been describing. It is this: the Dark Ages were the point during which there very gradually germinated and came into outward existence things which still remain among us and help to differentiate our Christendom from the past of classical antiquity.

This is true of certain material things. The spur, the double bridle, the stirrup, the book in leaves distinct from the old roll— and very much else. It is true of the road system of Europe wher-ever that road system has departed from the old Roman scheme. It was in the Dark Ages—with the gradual breakdown of expensive causeways over marshes, with the gradual decline of certain centers, with bridges left unrepaired, culverts choked and making a morass against the dam of the roads—that you got the deflection of the great ways. In almost every broad river valley in England, where an old Roman road crosses the stream and its low lying banks, you may see something which the Dark Ages left to us in our road system: you may see the modern road leaving the old Roman line and picking its way across the wet lands from one drier point to another, and rejoining the Roman line beyond. It is a thing you will see in almost any one of our Strettons, Stanfords, Stamfords, Staffords, etc., which everywhere mark the crossing of a Roman road over a water course.

But much more than in material things the Dark Ages set a mold wherein the European mind grew. For instance, it was they that gave to us two forms of legend. The one something older than history, older than the Roman order, something Western reappearing with the release of the mind from the rigid accuracy of a high civilization; the other that legend which preserves historical truth under a guise of phantasy.

Of the first, the British story of Tristan is one example out of a thousand. Of the second, the legend of Constantine, which gradually and unconsciously developed into the famous Donation.

The Dark Ages gave us that wealth of story coloring and enlivening all our European life, and what is more, largely preserving historic truth; for nothing is more valuable to true history than legend. They also gave us our order in speech. Great hosts of words unknown to antiquity sprang up naturally among the people when the force of the classical center failed. Some of them were words of the languages before the Roman armies came—cask, for instance, the old Iberian word. Some of them were the camp talk of the soldiers. Spade, for instance, and *"épée,"* the same piece of Greek slang, "the broad one," which has come to mean in French a sword, in English that with which we dig the earth. Masses of technical words in the old Roman laws turned into popular usage through that appetite the poor have for long official phrases: for instance, our English words *wild, weald, wold, waste, gain, rider, rode, ledge, say,* and a thousand others, all branch out from the lawyers' phrases of the later Roman Empire.

In this closed crucible of the Dark Ages crystallized also—by a process which we cannot watch, or of which we have but glimpses—that rich mass of jewels, the local customs of Europe, and even the local dress, which differentiates one place from another, when the communications of a high material civilization break down. In all this the Dark Ages are a comfort to the modern man, for he sees by their example that the process of increasing complexity reaches its term; that the strain of development is at last relieved; that humanity sooner or later returns upon itself; that there is an end in repose and that the repose is fruitful.

The last characteristic of the Dark Ages is that which has most engrossed, puzzled, and warped the judgment of non-Catholic historians when they have attempted a conspectus of European development; it was the segregation, the homogeneity of and the dominance of clerical organization.

The hierarchy of the Church, its unity and its sense of discipline was the chief civil institution and the chief binding social force of the times. Side by side with it went the establishment of the monastic institution, which everywhere took on a separate life of its own, preserved what could be preserved of arts and letters, drained the marshes and cleared the forests, and formed the ideal economic unit for such a period: almost the only economic unit in which capital could then be accumulated and preserved. The great order of St. Benedict formed a framework of living points upon which was stretched the moral life of Europe. The vast and increasing endowments of great and fixed religious houses formed the economic flywheel of those centuries. They were the granary and the storehouse. But for the monks, the fluctuations proceeding from raid and from decline would, in their violence, at some point or another, have snapped the chain of economic tradition, and we should all have fallen into barbarism.

Meanwhile the Catholic hierarchy as an institution—I have already called it by a violent metaphor, a civil institution—at any rate as a political institution—remained absolute above the social disintegration of the time.

All natural things were slowly growing up unchecked and disturbing the strict lines of the old centralized governmental order which men still remembered. In language Europe was a medley of infinitely varying local dialects.

Thousands upon thousands of local customs were coming to be separate laws in each separate village.

Legend, as I have said, was obscuring fixed history. The tribal basis from which we spring was thrusting its instincts back into the strict and rational Latin fabric of the State. Status was everywhere replacing contract, and habit replacing a reason for things. Above this medley the only absolute organization that could be was that of the Church. The Papacy was the one center whose shifting could not even be imagined. The Latin tongue, in the late form in which the Church used it, was everywhere the same, and everywhere suited to rituals that differed but slightly from province to province when we contrast them with the millioned diversity of local habit and speech.

Whenever a high civilization was to re-arise out of the soil of the Dark Ages, it was certain first to show a full organization of the Church under some Pope of exceptional vigor, and next to show that Pope, or his successors in this tradition, at issue with new civil powers. Whenever central government should rise again and in whatever form, a conflict would begin between the new kings and the clerical organization which had so strengthened itself during the Dark Ages.

Now Europe, as we know, did awake from its long sleep. The eleventh century was the moment of its awakening. Three great forces—the personality of St. Gregory VII, the appearance (by a happy accident of slight crossbreeding: a touch of Scandinavian blood added to the French race) of the Norman race, finally the Crusades—drew out of the darkness the enormous vigor of the early Middle Ages. They were to produce an intense and active civilization of their own; a civilization which was undoubtedly the highest and the best our race has known, conformable to the instincts of the European, fulfilling his nature, giving him that happiness which is the end of men.

As we also know, Europe on this great experiment of the Middle Ages, after four hundred years of high vitality, was rising to still greater heights when it suffered shipwreck.

With that disaster, the disaster of the Reformation, I shall deal later in this series.

In my next chapter I shall describe the inception of the Middle Ages, and show what they were before our promise in them was ruined.

7

THE MIDDLE AGES

I said in my last chapter that the Dark Ages might be compared to a long sleep of Europe: a sleep lasting from the fatigue of the old society in the fifth century to the spring and rising of the eleventh and twelfth. The metaphor is far too simple, of course, for that sleep was a sleep of war. In all those centuries Europe was desperately holding its own against the attack of all that desired to destroy it: refined and ardent Islam from the South, letterless barbarian pagans from the East and North. At any rate, from that sleep or that besieging Europe awoke or was relieved.

I said that three great forces, humanly speaking, worked this miracle; the personality of St. Gregory VII; the brief appearance, by a happy accident, of the Norman State; and finally the Crusades.

The Normans of history, the true French Normans we know, are stirring a generation after the year 1000. St. Gregory filled that same generation. He was a young man when the Norman effort began. He died, full of an enormous achievement, in 1085. As much as one man could, *he,* the heir of Cluny, had re-made Europe. Immediately after his death there was heard the march of the Crusades. From these three the vigor of a fresh, young, renewed Europe proceeds.

Much might be added. The perpetual and successful chivalric charge against the Mohammedan in Spain illumined all that time and clarified it. Asia was pushed back from the Pyrenees, and through the passes of the Pyrenees perpetually cavalcaded the high adventurers of Christendom. The Basques—a strange and very strong small people—were the pivot of that reconquest, but the valley of the torrent of the Aragon was its channel. The life of St. Gregory is contemporaneous with that of El Cid Campeador. In the same year that St. Gregory died, Toledo, the sacred center of Spain, was at last forced from the Mohammedans, and their Jewish allies, and firmly held. All Southern Europe was alive with the sword.

In that same moment romance appeared; the great songs: the greatest of them all, the Song of Roland; then was a ferment of the European mind, eager from its long repose, piercing into the undiscovered fields. That watching skepticism which flanks and follows the march of the Faith when the Faith is most vigorous had also begun to speak.

There was even some expansion beyond the boundaries eastward, so that something of the unfruitful Baltic Plain was reclaimed. Letters awoke, and Philosophy. Soon the greatest of all human exponents, St. Thomas Aquinas, was to appear. The plastic arts leapt up: Color and Stone. Humor fully returned: general travel: vision. In general, the moment was one of expectation and of advance. It was Spring.

For the purposes of these few pages I must confine the attention of my reader to those three tangible sources of the new Europe, which, as I have said, were the Normans, St. Gregory VII, and the Crusades.

Of the Norman race we may say that it resembled in history those *mirae* or new stars which flare out upon the darkness of the night sky for some few hours or weeks or years, and then are lost or merged in the infinity of things. He is indeed unhistorical who would pretend William the Conqueror, the organizer and maker of what we now call England, Robert the Wizard, the conquerors of Sicily, or any of the great Norman names that light Europe in the eleventh and twelfth centuries, to be even partly Scandinavians. They were Gauls: short in stature, lucid in design, vigorous in stroke, positive in philosophy. They bore no outward relation to the soft and tall and sentimental North from which some few of their remote ancestry had drawn ancestral names.

But on the other hand, anyone who should pretend that this amazing and ephemeral phenomenon, the Norman, was *merely* Gallo-Roman, would commit an error: an error far less gross but still misleading. In speech, in manner, in accoutrement, in the very trick of riding the horse, in the cooking of food, in that most intimate part of man, his jests, the Norman was wholly and apparently a Gaul. In his body—hard, short, square, broad-shouldered, alert—the Norman was a Frenchman only. But no other part of Gaul *then* did what Normandy did: nor could any other French province show, as Normandy showed, immediate, organized and creative power, during the few years that the marvel lasted.

That marvel is capable of explanation and I will attempt to explain it. Those dull, blundering and murderous ravagings of the coasts of Christian Europe by the pirates of Scandinavia (few in number, futile in achievement) which we call in English history, "The Danish Invasions," were called upon the opposite coast of the Channel, "The Invasions of the Nordmanni" or "the Men of the North." They came from the Baltic and from Norway. They were part of the universal assault which the Dark Ages of Christendom had to sustain: part of a ceaseless pressure from without against civilization; and they were but a part of it. They were few, as pirates always must be. It was on the estuaries of a few continental rivers and in the British Isles that they counted most in the lives of Europeans.

Now among the estuaries of the great rivers was the estuary of the Seine. The Scandinavian pirates forced it again and again. At the end of the ninth century they had besieged Paris, which was then rapidly becoming the political center of Gaul.

So much was there left of the Roman tradition in that last stronghold of the Roman Empire that the quieting of invading hordes by their settlement (by inter-marriage with and granting of land in, a fixed Roman province) was a policy still obvious to those who still called themselves "The Emperors" of the West.

In the year 911 this antique method, consecrated by centuries of tradition, produced its last example and the barbarian troublers from the sea were given a fixed limit of land wherein they might settle. The maritime province "Lugdunensis Secunda"[21] was handed over to them for settlement, that is, they might not attempt a partition of the land outside its boundaries.

On the analogy of all similar experiments we can be fairly certain of what happened, though there is no contemporary record of such domestic details in the case of Normandy.

The barbarians, few in number, coming into a fertile and thickly populated Roman province, only slightly affected its blood, but their leaders occupied waste land, planted themselves as heirs of existing childless lords, took to wife the heiresses of others; enfeoffed groups of small men; took a share of the revenue; helped to answer for military levy and general government. Their chief was responsible to the crown.

To the mass of the population the new arrangement would make no change; they were no longer slaves, but they were still serfs. Secure of their small farms, but still bound to work for their lord, it mattered little to them whether that lord of theirs had married his daughter to a pirate or had made a pirate his heir or his partner in the management of the estate. All the change the serf would notice from the settlement was that the harrying and the plundering of occasional barbarian raids had ceased.

In the governing class of perhaps some ten to twenty thousand families the difference would be very noticeable indeed. The pirate newcomers, though insignificant in number compared with the total population, were a very large fraction added to so small a body. The additional blood, though numerically a small proportion, permeated rapidly throughout the whole community. Scandinavian names and habits may have had at first some little effect upon the owner-class with which the Scandinavians first mingled; it soon disappeared. But, as had been the

---

21. The delimitation of this province dated from Diocletian. It was already six hundred years old; its later name of "Normandy" masked this essential fact that it was and is a Roman division, as for that matter are probably our English counties.

case centuries before in the earlier experiments of that sort, it was the barbarian chief and his hereditary descendants who took over the local government and "held it," as the phrase went, of the universal government of Gaul.

These "North-men," the new and striking addition to the province, the Gallo-Romans called, as we have seen, "Nordmanni." The Roman province, within the limits of which they were strictly settled, the second Lyonnese, came to be called "Normannia." For a century the slight admixture of new blood worked in the general Gallo-Roman mass of the province and, numerically small though it was, influenced its character, or rather produced a new thing; just as in certain chemical combinations the small admixture of a new element transforms the whole. With the beginning of the eleventh century, as everything was springing into new life, when the great saint who, from the chair of Peter, was to restore the Church was already born, when the advance of the Pyreneans against Islam was beginning to strike its decisive conquering blows, there appeared a sudden phenomenon, this new thing—French in speech and habit and disposition of body, yet just differentiated from the rest of Frenchmen—*the Norman Race.*

It possessed these characteristics—a great love of exact order, an alert military temper and a passion for reality which made its building even of ships (though it was not in the main seafaring) excellent, and of churches and of castles the most solid of its time.

All the Normans' characteristics (once the race was formed) led them to advance. They conquered England and organized it; they conquered and organized Sicily and Southern Italy; they made of Normandy itself the model state in a confused time; they surveyed land; they developed a regular tactic for mailed cavalry. Yet they endured for but a hundred years, and after that brief coruscation they are wholly merged again in the mass of European things!

You may take the first adventurous lords of the Cotentin in, say 1030, for the beginning of the Norman thing; you may take the Court of young Henry II, with his Southerners and his high culture in, say 1160, most certainly for the burial of it. During that little space of time the Norman had not only reintroduced exactitude in the government of men, he had also provided the sword of the new Papacy and he had furnished the framework of the crusading host. But before his adventure was done the French language and the writ of Rome ran from the Grampians to the Euphrates.

Of the Papacy and the Crusades I now speak.

St. Gregory VII, the second of the great re-creative forces of that time, was of the Tuscan peasantry, Etrurian in type, therefore Italian in speech, by name Hildebrand. Whether an historian understands his career or no is a very test of whether that historian understands the nature of Europe. For St. Gregory VII imposed nothing upon Europe. He made nothing new. What he did was to stiffen the ideal with reality. He provoked a resurrection of the flesh. He made corporate the centralized Church and the West.

For instance, it was the ideal, the doctrine, the tradition, the major custom by far, that the clergy should be celibate. He enforced celibacy as universal discipline.

The awful majesty of the Papacy had been present in all men's minds as a vast political conception for centuries too long to recall; St. Gregory organized that monarchy, and gave it proper instruments of rule.

The Unity of the Church had been the constant image without which Christendom could not be; St. Gregory VII at every point made that unity tangible and visible. The Protestant historians who, for the most part, see in the man a sporadic phenomenon, by such a misconception betray the source of their anemia and prove their intellectual nourishment to be unfed from the fountain of European life. St. Gregory VII was not an inventor, but a renovator. He worked not upon, but in, his material; and his material was the nature of Europe: our nature.

Of the awful obstacles such workers must encounter all history speaks. They are at conflict not only with evil, but with inertia; and with local interest, with blurred vision and with restricted landscapes. Always they think themselves defeated, as did St.

Gregory when he died. Always they prove themselves before posterity to have done much more than any other mold of man. Napoleon also was of this kind.

When St. Gregory was dead the Europe which he left was the monument of that triumph whose completion he had doubted and the fear of whose failure had put upon his dying lips the phrase: "I have loved justice and hated iniquity, therefore I die in exile."

Immediately after his death came the stupendous Gallic effort of the Crusades.

The Crusades were the second of the main armed eruptions of the Gauls. The first, centuries before, had been the Gallic invasion of Italy and Greece and the Mediterranean shores in the old Pagan time. The third, centuries later, was to be the wave of the Revolution and of Napoleon.

The preface to the Crusades appeared in those endless and already successful wars of Christendom against Asia upon the high plateaus of Spain. *These* had taught the enthusiasm and the method by which Asia, for so long at high tide flooding a beleaguered Europe, might be slowly repelled, and from *these* had proceeded the military science and the aptitude for strain which made possible the advance of two thousand miles upon the Holy Land. The consequences of this last and third factor in the re-awakening of Europe were so many that I can give but a list of them here.

The West, still primitive, discovered through the Crusades the intensive culture, the accumulated wealth, the fixed civilized traditions of the Greek Empire and of the town of Constantinople. It discovered also, in a vivid new experience, the East. The mere covering of so much land, the mere seeing of so many sights by a million men expanded and broke the walls of the mind of the Dark Ages. The Mediterranean came to be covered with Christian ships, and took its place again with fertile rapidity as the great highway of exchange.

Europe awoke. All architecture is transformed, and that quite new thing, the Gothic, arises. The conception of representative assembly, monastic in origin, fruitfully transferred to civilian soil, appears in the institutions of Christendom. The vernacular languages appear, and with them the beginnings of our literature: the Tuscan, the Castilian, the Langue d'Oc, the Northern French, somewhat later the English. Even the primitive tongues that had always kept their vitality from beyond recorded time, the Celtic and the German,[22] begin to take on new creative powers and to produce a new literature. That fundamental institution of Europe, the University, arises; first in Italy, immediately after in Paris—which last becomes the type and center of the scheme.

The central civil governments begin to correspond to their natural limits; the English monarchy is fixed first, the French kingdom is coalescing, the Spanish regions will soon combine. The Middle Ages are born.

The flower of that capital experiment in the history of our race was the thirteenth century. Edward I of England, St. Louis of France, Pope Innocent III, were the types of its governing manhood. Everywhere Europe was renewed; there were new white walls around the cities, new white Gothic churches in the towns, new castles on the hills, law codified, the classics rediscovered, the questions of philosophy sprung to activity and producing in their first vigor, as it were, the summit of expository power in St. Thomas, surely the strongest, the most virile, intellect which our European blood has given to the world.

Two notes mark the time for anyone who is acquainted with its building, its letters, and its wars: a note of youth, and a note of content. Europe was imagined to be at last achieved, and that ineradicable dream of a permanent and satisfactory society seemed to have taken on flesh and to have come to live forever among Christian men.

---

22. I mean, in neither of the groups of tongues as we first find them recorded, for by that time each—especially the German—was full of Southern words borrowed from the Empire; but the original stocks which survived side by side with this new vocabulary. For instance, our first knowledge of Teutonic dialect is of the eighth century (the so-called Early Gothic is a fraud) but even then quite half the words or more are truly German, apparently unaffected by the Imperial laws and speech.

No such permanence and no such good is permitted to humanity; and the great experiment, as I have called it, was destined to fail.

While it flourished, all that is specially characteristic of our European descent and nature stood visibly present in the daily life, and in the large, as in the small, institutions of Europe.

Our property in land and instruments was well divided among many or all; we produced the peasant; we maintained the independent craftsman; we founded cooperative industry. In arms that military type arose which lives upon the virtues proper to arms and detests the vices arms may breed. Above all, an intense and living appetite for truth, a perception of reality, invigorated these generations. They saw what was before them, they called things by their names. Never was political or social formula less divorced from fact, never was the mass of our civilization better welded—and in spite of all this the thing did not endure.

By the middle of the fourteenth century the decaying of the flower was tragically apparent. New elements of cruelty tolerated, of mere intrigue successful, of emptiness in philosophical phrase and of sophistry in philosophical argument, marked the turn of the tide. Not an institution of the thirteenth but the fourteenth debased it; the Papacy professional and a prisoner, the parliaments tending to oligarchy, the popular ideals dimmed in the minds of the rulers, the new and vigorous and democratic monastic orders already touched with mere wealth and beginning also to change—but these last can always, and do always, restore themselves.

Upon all this came the enormous incident of the Black Death. Here half the people, there a third, there again a quarter, died; from that additional blow the great experiment of the Middle Ages could not recover.

Men clung to their ideal for yet another hundred and fifty years. The vital forces it had developed still carried Europe from one material perfection to another; the art of government, the suggestion of letters, the technique of sculpture and of painting (here raised by a better vision, there degraded by a worse one) everywhere developed and grew manifold. But the supreme achievement of the thirteenth century was seen in the later fourteenth to be ephemeral, and in the fifteenth it was apparent that the attempt to found a simple and satisfied Europe had failed.

The full causes of that failure cannot be analyzed. One may say that science and history were too slight; that the material side of life was insufficient; that the full knowledge of the past which is necessary to permanence was lacking—or one may say that the ideal was too high for men. I, for my part, incline to believe that wills other than those of mortals were in combat for the soul of Europe, as they are in combat daily for the souls of individual men, and that in this spiritual battle, fought over our heads perpetually, some accident of the struggle turned it against us for a time. If that suggestion be fantastic (which no doubt it is), at any rate none other is complete.

With the end of the fifteenth century there was to come a supreme test and temptation. The fall of Constantinople and the release of Greek: the rediscovery of the Classic past: the Press: the new great voyages—India to the East, America to the West— had (in the one lifetime of a man[23] between 1453 and 1515) suddenly brought Europe into a new, a magic, and a dangerous land.

To the provinces of Europe, shaken by an intellectual tempest of physical discovery, disturbed by an abrupt and undigested enlargement in the material world, in physical science, and in the knowledge of antiquity, was to be offered a fruit of which each might taste if it would, but the taste of which would lead, if it were acquired, to evils no citizen of Europe then dreamt of; to things which even the criminal intrigues and the cruel tyrants of the fifteenth century would have shuddered to contemplate, and to a disaster which very nearly overset our ship of history and very nearly lost us forever its cargo of letters, of

---

23. The lifetime of one very great and famous man did cover it. Ferdinand, King of Aragon, the mighty Spaniard, the father of the noblest of English queens, was born the year before Constantinople fell. He died the year before Luther found himself swept to the head of a chaotic wave.

philosophy, of the arts, and of all our other powers.

That disaster is commonly called "The Reformation." I do not pretend to analyze its material causes, for I doubt if any of its causes were wholly material. I rather take the shape of the event and show how the ancient and civilized boundaries of Europe stood firm, though shaken, under the tempest; how that tempest might have ravaged no more than those outlying parts newly incorporated—never sufficiently penetrated perhaps with the Faith and the proper habits of ordered men—the outer Germanies and Scandinavia.

The disaster would have been upon a scale not too considerable, and Europe might quickly have righted herself after the gust should be passed, had not one exception of capital amount marked the intensest crisis of the storm. That exception to the resistance offered by the rest of ancient Europe was the defection of Britain.

Conversely with this loss of an ancient province of the Empire, one nation, and one alone, of those which the Roman Empire had not bred, stood the strain and preserved the continuity of Christian tradition: that nation was Ireland.

8

WHAT WAS THE REFORMATION?

This is perhaps the greatest of all historical questions, after the original question: "What was the Church in the Empire of Rome?" A true answer to this original question gives the nature of that capital revolution by which Europe came to unity and to maturity and attained to a full consciousness of itself. An answer to the other question: "What was the Reformation?" begins to explain our modern ill-ease.

A true answer to the question: "What was the Reformation?" is of such vast importance, because it is only when we grasp *what the Reformation was* that we understand its consequences. Then only do we know how the united body of European civilization has been cut asunder and by what a wound. The abomination of industrialism; the loss of land and capital by the people in great districts of Europe; the failure of modern discovery to serve the end of man; the series of larger and still larger wars following in a rapidly rising scale of severity and destruction—till the dead are now counted in tens of millions; the increasing chaos and misfortune of society—all these attach one to the other, each falls into its place, and a hundred smaller phenomena as well, when we appreciate, as today we can, the nature and the magnitude of that fundamental catastrophe.

It is possible that the perilous business is now drawing to its end, and that (though those now living will not live to see it) Christendom may enter into a convalescence: may at last forget the fever and be restored. With that I am not here concerned. It is my business only to explain that storm which struck Europe four hundred years ago and within a century

154

brought Christendom to shipwreck.

The true causes are hidden—for they were spiritual.

In proportion as an historical matter is of import to human kind, in that proportion does it spring not from apparent—let alone material—causes, but from some hidden revolution in the human spirit. To pretend an examination of the secret springs whence the human mind is fed is futile. The greater the affair, the more directly does it proceed from unseen sources which the theologian may catalogue, the poet see in vision, the philosopher explain, but with which positive external history cannot deal, and which the mere historian cannot handle. It is the function of history to present the outward thing, as a witness might have seen it, and to show the reader as much as a spectator could have seen—illuminated indeed by a knowledge of the past—and a judgment drawn from known succeeding events. The historian answers the question, "*What* was?" this or that. To the question, "*Why* was it?" if it be in the spiritual order (as are all major things), the reader must attempt his own reply based upon other aptitudes than those of historic science.

It is the neglect of this canon which makes barren so much work upon the past. Read Gibbon's attempt to account for "why" the Catholic Church arose in the Roman Empire, and mark his empty failure.[24]

Mark also how all examination of the causes of the French Revolution are colored by something small and degraded, quite out of proportion to that stupendous crusade which transformed the modern world. The truth is, that the historian can only detail those causes, largely material, all evident and positive, which lie within his province, and such causes are quite insufficient to explain the full result. Were I here writing "Why" the

---

24. It is true that Gibbon was ill-equipped for his task because he lacked historical imagination. He could not grasp the spirit of a past age. He could not enter into any mood save that of his master, Voltaire. But it is not only true of Gibbon that he fails to explain the great revolution of A.D. 29-304. No one attempting that explanation has succeeded. It was not of this world.

Reformation came, my reply would not be historic, but mystic. I should say that it came "from outside mankind." But that would be to affirm without the hope of proof, and only in the confidence that all attempts at positive proof were contemptible. Luckily I am not concerned in so profound an issue, but only in the presentation of the thing as it was. Upon this I now set out.

With the close of the Middle Ages two phenomena appeared side by side in the society of Europe. The first was an ageing and a growing fatigue of the simple mediaeval scheme; the second was a very rapid accretion of technical power.

As to the first I have suggested (it is no more than a suggestion) that the mediaeval scheme of society, though much the best fitted to our race and much the best expression which it has yet found, though especially productive of happiness (which here and hereafter is the end of man), was not properly provided with instruments of survival.

Its science was too imperfect, its institutions too local, though its philosophy was the widest ever framed and the most satisfying to the human intelligence.

Whatever be the reason, that society *did* rapidly grow old. Its every institution grew formal or debased. The Guilds from true cooperative partnerships for the proper distribution of the means of production, and for the prevention of a proletariat with its vile cancer of capitalism, tended to become privileged bodies. Even the heart of Christian Europe, the village, showed faint signs that it might become an oligarchy of privileged farmers with some land and less men at their orders. The Monastic orders were tainted in patches up and down Europe, with worldliness, with an abandonment of their strict rule, and occasionally with vice. Civil government grew befogged with tradition and with complex rules. All manner of theatrical and false trappings began to deform society, notably the exaggeration of heraldry and a riot of symbolism of which very soon no one could make head or tail.

The temporal and visible organization of the Church did not escape in such a welter. The lethargy, avarice, and routine from which that organization suffered has been both grossly exaggerated and set out of perspective. A wild picture of it has been drawn by its enemies. But in a degree the temporal organization of the Church had decayed at the close of the Middle Ages. It was partly too much a taking of things for granted, a conviction that nothing could really upset the unity of Europe; partly the huge concentration of wealth in clerical hands, which proceeded from the new economic activity all over Europe, coupled with the absolute power of the clergy in certain centers and the universal economic function of Rome; partly a popular loss of faith. All these between them helped to do the business. At any rate, the evil was there.

All institutions (says Machiavelli) must return to their origins, or they fail. There appeared throughout Europe in the last century of united Europe, breaking out here and there, sporadic attempts to revivify the common life, especially upon its spiritual side, by a return to the primitive communal enthusiasms in which religion necessarily has its historical origins.

This was in no way remarkable. Neither was it remarkable that each such sporadic and spontaneous outburst should have its own taint or vice or false color.

What was remarkable and what made the period unique in the whole history of Christendom (save for the Arian flood) was the incapacity of the external organization of the Church at the moment to capture the spiritual discontent, and to satisfy the spiritual hunger of which these errors were the manifestation.

In a slower time the external organization of the Church would have absorbed and regulated the new things, good and evil. It would have rendered the heresies ridiculous in turn, it would have canalized the exaltations, it would have humanized the discoveries. But things were moving at a rate more and more rapid, the whole society of Western Christendom raced from experience to experience. It was flooded with the newly found manuscripts of antiquity, with the new discoveries of unknown continents, with new commerce, printing, and, an effect perhaps rather than a cause, the complete rebirth of painting, architecture, sculpture and all the artistic expression of Europe.

In point of fact, this doubt and seething and attempted return to early religious enthusiasm were not digested and were not captured. The spiritual hunger of the time was not fed. Its extravagance was not exposed to the solvent of laughter or to the flame of a sufficient indignation: they were therefore neither withered nor eradicated. For the spirit had grown old. The great movement of the spirit in Europe was repressed haphazard and, quite as much haphazard, encouraged, but there seemed no one corporate force present throughout Christendom which would persuade, encourage and command: even the Papacy, the core of our unity, was shaken by long division and intrigue.

Let it be clearly understood that in the particular form of special heresies the business was local, peculiar and contemptible. Wycliffe, for instance, was no more the morning star of the Reformation than Catherine of Braganza's Tangier Dowry, let us say, was the morning star of the modern English Empire. Wycliffe was but one of a great number of men who were theorizing up and down Europe upon the nature of society and morals, each with his special metaphysic of the Sacrament; each with his "system." Such men have always abounded; they abound today. Some of Wycliffe's extravagances resemble what many Protestants happen, later, to have held; others (such as his theory that you could not own land unless you were in a state of grace) were of the opposite extreme to Protestantism. And so it is with the whole lot: and there were hundreds of them. There was no common theory, no common feeling in the various reactions against a corrupted ecclesiastical authority which marked the end of the Middle Ages. There was nothing the least like what we call Protestantism today. Indeed, that spirit and mental color does not appear until a couple of generations after the opening of the Reformation itself.

What there *was,* was a widespread discontent and exasperated friction against the existing, rigid, and yet deeply decayed, temporal organization of religious affairs; and in their uneasy fretting against that unworthy rule, the various centers of irritation put up now one startling theory which they knew would annoy the official Church, now another, perhaps the exact opposite of the last. Now they denied something as old as Europe—such as the right to property: now a new piece of usage or discipline such as Communion in one kind: now a partial regional rule, such as celibacy. Some went stark mad. Others, at the contrary extreme, did no more than expose false relics.

A general social ill-ease was the parent of all these sporadic heresies. Many had elaborate systems, but none of these systems was a true creed, that is, a *motive*. No one of the outbursts had any philosophic driving power behind it; all and each were no more than violent and blind reactions against a clerical authority which gave scandal and set up an intolerable strain.

Shall I give an example? One of the most popular forms which the protest took was what I have just mentioned, a demand for Communion in both kinds and for the restoration of what was in many places ancient custom, the drinking from the cup after the priest.

Could anything better prove the truth that mere irritation against the external organization of the Church was the power at work? Could any point have less to do with the fundamentals of the Faith? Of course, as an *implication* of false doctrine—as that the Priesthood is not an Order, or that the Presence of Our Lord is not in both species—it had its importance. But in itself how trivial a "kick." Why should anyone desire the cup, save to mark dissension from established custom!

Here is another example. Prominent among the later expressions of discontent you have the Adamites,[25] who among other tenets rejected clothes upon the more solemn occasions of their ritual and went naked: raving maniacs. The whole business was

---

25. The rise of these oddities is nearly contemporary with Wycliffe and is, like his career, about one hundred years previous to the Reformation proper: the sects are of various longevity. Some, like the Calvinists, have, while dwindling rapidly in numbers, kept their full doctrines for now four hundred years; others, like the Johanna Southcottites, hardly last a lifetime: others, like the Modernists, a decade or less [though Modernism resurfaced in the 1960's]: others, like the Mormons, near a century: their close is not yet. I myself met a man in Colorado in 1891 whose friends thought him the Messiah. Unlike the Wycliffites, certain members of the Adamites until lately survived in Austria.

a rough and tumble of protest against the breakdown of a social system whose breakdown seemed the more terrible because it *had* been such a haven! Because it *was* in essence founded upon the most intimate appetites of European men. The heretics were angry because they had lost their home.

This very general picture omits Huss and the national movement for which he stood. It omits the Papal Schism; the Council of Constance; all the great facts of the fifteenth century on its religious side. I am concerned only with the presentation of the general character of the time, and that character was what I have described: an irrepressible, largely justified, discontent breaking out: a sort of chronic rash upon the skin of Christian Europe, which rash the body of Christendom could neither absorb nor cure.

Now at this point—and before we leave the fifteenth century—there is another historical feature which it is of the utmost importance to seize if we are to understand what followed; for it was a feature common to all European thought until a time long after the final establishment of permanent cleavage in Europe. It is a feature which nearly all historians neglect, and yet one manifest upon the reading of any contemporary expression. That feature is this: *No one in the Reformation dreamt a divided Christendom to be possible.*

This flood of heretical movement was *oecumenical;* it was not peculiar to one race or climate or culture or nation. The numberless uneasy innovators thought, even the wildest of them, in terms of Europe as a whole. They desired to affect the universal Church and change it *en bloc.* They had no local ambition. They stood for no particular blood or temperament; they sprang up everywhere, bred by the universal ill-ease of a society still universal. You were as likely to get an enthusiast declaring himself to be the Messiah in Seville as an enthusiast denying the Real Presence in Aberdeen.

That fatal habit of reading into the past what we know of its future has in this matter most deplorably marred history, and men, whether Protestant or Catholic, who are now accustomed to Protestantism, read Protestantism and the absurd idea of a local religion—a religion true in one place and untrue in another—into a time where the least instructed clown would have laughed in your face at such nonsense.

The whole thing, the evil coupled with a quite ineffectual resistance to the evil, was a thing common to all Europe.

It is the nature of any organic movement to progress or to recede. But this movement was destined to advance with devastating rapidity, and that on account of what I have called the *second* factor in the Reformation: the very rapid accretion in technical power which marked the close of the Middle Ages.

Printing; navigation; all mensuration; the handling of metals and every material—all these took a sudden leap forward with the *Renaissance,* the revival of arts: that vast stirring of the later Middle Ages which promised to give us a restored antiquity Christianized: which was burnt in the flame of a vile fanaticism, and has left us nothing but ashes and incommiscible salvage.

Physical knowledge, the expansion of physical experience and technical skill, were moving in the century before the Reformation at such a rate that a contemporary spiritual phenomenon, if it advanced at all, was bound to advance very rapidly, and this spiritual eruption in Europe came to a head just at the moment when the contemporary expansion of travel, of economic activity and of the revival of learning had also emerged in their full force.

It was in the first twenty years of the sixteenth century that the coalescing of the various forces of spiritual discontent and revolt began to be apparent. Before 1530 the general storm was to burst and the Reformation proper to be started on its way.

But as a preliminary to that matter, the reader should first understand how another and quite disconnected social development had prepared the way for the triumph of the reformers. This development was the advent of Absolute Government in civil affairs.

Here and there in the long history of Europe there crops up an isolated accident, very striking, very effective, of short duration. We have already seen that the Norman race was one of these. Tyranny in civil government (which accompanied the

Reformation) was another.

A claim to absolute monarchy is one of the commonest and most enduring of historical things. Countless centuries of the old Empires of the East were passed under such a claim, the Roman Empire was based upon it; the old Russian State was made by it, French society luxuriated in it for one magnificent century, from the accession of Louis XIV till Fontenoy. It is the easiest and (when it works) the most prompt of all instruments.

But the sense of an absolute civil government at the moment of the Reformation was something very different. It was a demand, an appetite, proceeding from the whole community, a worship of civil authority. It was deification of the State and of law; it was the adoration of the Executive.

"This governs me; therefore I will worship it and do all it tells me." Such is the formula for the strange passion which has now and then seized great bodies of human beings intoxicated by splendor and by the vivifying effects of command. Like all manias (for it is a mania) this exaggerated passion is hardly comprehended once it is past. Like all manias, while it is present it overrides every other emotion.

Europe, in the time of which I speak, suffered such a mania. The free cities manifested that disease quite as much as the great monarchical states. In Rome itself the temporal power of the Papal sovereign was then magnificent beyond all past parallel. In Geneva Calvin was a god. In Spain Charles and Philip governed two worlds without question. In England the Tudor dynasty was worshipped blindly. Men might and did rebel against a particular government, but it was only to set up something equally absolute in its place. Not the form, but the fact of government was adored.

I will not waste the reader's time in any discussion upon the causes of that astonishing political fever. It must suffice to say that for a moment it hypnotized the whole world. It would have been incomprehensible to the Middle Ages. It was incomprehensible to the nineteenth century. It wholly occupied the sixteenth. If we understand it, we largely understand what made the success of the Reformation possible.

Well, then, the increasing discontent of the masses against the decaying forms of the Middle Ages, and the increasing irritation against the temporal government and the organization of the Church, came to a head just at that moment when civil government was worshipped as an awful and almost divine thing.

Into such an atmosphere was launched the last and the strongest of the overt protests against the old social scheme, and in particular against the existing power of the Papacy, especially upon its economic side.

The name most prominently associated with the crisis is that of Martin Luther, an Augustinian monk, German by birth and speech, and one of those exuberant, sensual, rather inconsequential, characters which so easily attract hearty friendships, and which can never pretend to organization or command, though certainly to creative power. What he precisely meant or would do, no man could tell, least of all himself. He was "out" for protest and he floated on the crest of the general wave of change. That he ever intended, nay, that he could ever have imagined, a disruption of the European Unity is impossible.

Luther (a voice, no leader) was but one of many: had he never lived, the great bursting wave would have crashed onward much the same. One scholar after another (and these of every blood and from every part of Europe) joined in the upheaval. The opposition of the old monastic training to the newly revived classics, of the ascetic to the new pride of life, of the logician to the mystic, all these in a confused whirl swept men of every type into the disruption. One thing only united them. They were all inflamed with a vital necessity for change. Great names which in the ultimate challenge refused to destroy and helped to preserve—the greatest is that of Erasmus; great names which even appear in the roll of that of the Catholic martyrs—the blessed Thomas More is the greatest of these—must here be counted with the names of men like the narrow Calvin on the one hand, the large Rabelais upon the other. Not one ardent mind in the first half of the sixteenth century but was swept into the stream.

Now all this would and must have been quieted in the process of time, the mass of Christendom would have settled back into unity, the populace would have felt instinctively the risk they ran of spoliation by the rich and powerful, if the popular institutions of Christendom broke down: the masses would have all swung round to solidifying society after an upheaval (it is their function): we should have attained repose, and Europe, united again, would have gone forward as she did after the rocking of four hundred years before—but for that other factor of which I have spoken, the passion which this eager creative moment felt for the absolute in civil government—that craving for the something godlike which makes men worship a flag, a throne or a national hymn.

This it was which caught up and, in the persons of particular men, used the highest of the tide. Certain princes in the Germanies (who had, of all the groups of Europe, least grasped the meaning of authority) befriended here one heresiarch and there another. The very fact that the Pope of Rome stood for one of these absolute governments put other absolute governments against him. The wind of the business rose; it became a quarrel of sovereigns. And the sovereigns decided, and powerful usurping nobles or leaders decided, the future of the herd.

Two further characters appeared side by side in the earthquake that was breaking up Europe.

The first was this: the tendency to fall away from European unity seemed more and more marked in those outer places which lay beyond the original limits of the old Roman Empire, and notably in the Northern Netherlands and in Northern Germany— where men easily submitted to the control of wealthy merchants and of hereditary landlords.

The second was this: a profound distrust of the new movement, a reaction against it, a feeling that moral anarchy was too profitable to the rich and the cupidinous, began at first in a dull, later in an angry way, to stir the masses of the populace throughout *all* Christendom.

The stronger the old Latin sense of human equality was, the more the populace felt this, the more they instinctively conceived of the Reformation as something that would rob them of some ill-understood but profound spiritual guarantee against slavery, exploitation and oppression.

There began a sort of popular grumbling against the Reformers, who were now already schismatic: their rich patrons fell under the same suspicion. By the time the movement had reached a head and by the time the central power of the Church had been openly defied by the German princes, this protest took, as in France and England and the valley of the Rhone (the ancient seats of culture), a noise like the undertone of the sea before bad weather. In the outer Germanies it was not a defense of Christendom at all, but a brutish cry for more food. But everywhere the populace stirred.

A general observer, cognizant of what was to come, would have been certain at that moment that the populace would rise. When it rose *intelligently*, the movement against the Church and civilization would come to nothing. The Revolt elsewhere—in half barbaric Europe—would come to no more than the lopping off of outer and insignificant things. The Baltic Plain, sundry units of the outer Germanies and Scandinavia, probably Hungary, possibly Bohemia, certain mountain valleys in Switzerland and Savoy and France and the Pyrenees, which had suffered from lack of instruction and could easily be recovered—these would be affected. The outer parts, which had never been within the pale of the Roman Empire, might go. But the soul and intelligence of Europe would be kept sound; its general body would reunite and Christendom would once more reappear whole and triumphant. It would have reconquered these outer parts at its leisure: and Poland was a sure bastion. We should, within a century, have been ourselves once more: Christian men.

So it would have been—but for one master tragedy, which changed the whole scheme. Of the four great remaining units of Western civilization—Iberia, Italy, Britain and Gaul—one, at this critical moment, broke down by a tragic accident and lost continuity. It was hardly intended. It was a consequence of error much more than an act of will. But it had full effect.

The breakdown of Britain and her failure to resist disruption was the chief event of all. It made the Reformation permanent. It confirmed a final division in Europe.

By a curious accident, one province, extraneous to the Empire, Ireland, heroically preserved what the other extraneous provinces, the Germanies and Scandinavia, were to lose. In spite of the loss of Britain, and cut off by that loss from direct succor, Ireland preserved the tradition of civilization.

It must be my next business to describe the way in which Britain failed in the struggle, and, at the hands of the King, and of a little group of avaricious men (such as the Howards among the gentry, and the Cecils among the adventurers) changed for the worse the history of Europe.

9

THE DEFECTION OF BRITAIN

One thing stands out in the fate of modern Europe: the profound cleavage due to the Reformation. One thing made that wound (it was almost mortal) so deep and *lasting:* the failure of one ancient province of civilization, and one only, to keep the Faith: this province whereof I write: Britain.

The capital event, the critical moment, in the great struggle of the Faith against the Reformation, was the defection of Britain.

It is a point which the modern historian, who is still normally anti-Catholic, does not and cannot make. Yet the defection of Britain from the Faith of Europe three hundred years ago is certainly the most important historical event in the last thousand years: between the saving of Europe from the barbarians and these our own times. It is perhaps the most important historical event since the triumph of the Catholic Church under Constantine.

Let me recapitulate the factors of the problem as they would be seen by an impartial observer from some great distance in time, or in space, or in mental attitude. Let me put them as they would appear to one quite indifferent to, and remote from, the antagonists.

To such an observer the history of Europe would be that of the great Roman Empire passing through the transformation I have described: its mind first more and more restless, then more and more tending to a certain conclusion, and that conclusion the Catholic Church.

To summarize what has gone before: the Catholic Church

becomes by the fifth century the soul, the vital principle, the continuity of Europe. It next suffers grievously from the accident, largely geographical, of the Eastern schism. It is of its nature perpetually subject to assault; from within, because it deals with matters not open to positive proof; from without, because all those, whether aliens or guests or parasites, who are not of our civilization, are naturally its enemies.

The Roman empire of the West, in which the purity and unity of this soul were preserved from generation to generation, declined in its body during the Dark Ages—say, up to and rather beyond the year 1000. It became coarsened and less in its material powers. It lost its central organization, the Imperial Court (which was replaced first by provincial military leaders or "kings," then, later, by a mass of local lordships jumbled into more or less national groups). In building, in writing, in cooking, in clothing, in drawing, in sculpture, the Roman Empire of the West (which is ourselves) forgot all but the fundamentals of its arts—but it expanded so far as its area is concerned. A whole belt of barbaric Germany received the Roman influence—Baptism and the Mass. With the Creed there came to these outer parts reading and writing, building in brick and stone—all the material essentials of our civilization—and what is characteristic of that culture, the power of thinking more clearly.

It is centuries before this slow digestion of the barbarian reached longitude ten degrees east, and the Scandinavian peninsula. But a thousand years after Our Lord it has reached even these, and there remains between the unbroken tradition of our civilization in the West and the schismatic but Christian civilization of the Greek Church, nothing but a belt of paganism from the corner of the Baltic southward, which belt is lessened, year after year, by the armed efforts and the rational dominance of Latin culture. Our Christian and Roman culture proceeds continuously eastward, mastering the uncouth.

After this general picture of a civilization dominating and mastering in its material decline a vastly greater area than it had known in the height of its material excellence—this sort of expansion in the dark—the impartial observer, whom we have supposed, would remark a sort of dawn.

That dawn came with the eleventh century: 1000-1100. The Norman race, the sudden invigoration of the Papacy, the new victories in Spain, at last the first Crusade, mark a turn in the tide of material decline, and that tide works very rapidly towards a new and intense civilization which we call that of the Middle Ages: that high renewal which gives Europe a second and most marvelous life, which is a late reflowering of Rome, but of Rome revivified with the virtue and the humor of the Faith.

The second thing that the observer would note in so general a picture would be the peculiar exception formed within it by the group of large islands lying to the North and West of the Continent. Of these the larger, Britain, had been a true Roman Province; but very early in the process—in the middle and end of the fifth century—it had on the first assault of the barbarians been cut off for more than the lifetime of a man. Its gate had been held by the barbarian. Then it was re-Christianized almost as thoroughly as though even its Eastern part had never lost the authority of civilization. The Mission of St. Augustine recaptured Britain—but Britain is remarkable in the history of civilization for the fact that alone of civilized lands it needed to be recaptured at all. The western island of the two, the smaller island, Ireland, presented another exception.

It was not compelled to the Christian culture, as were the German barbarians of the Continent, by arms. No Charlemagne with his Gallic armies forced it tardily to accept baptism. It was not savage like the Germanies; it was therefore under no necessity to go to school. It was not a morass of shifting tribes; it was a nation. But in a most exceptional fashion, though already possessed, and perhaps because so possessed, of a high pagan culture of its own, it accepted within the lifetime of a man, and by spiritual influences alone, the whole spirit of the Creed. The civilization of the Roman West was accepted by Ireland, not as a command nor as an influence, but as a discovery.

Now let this peculiar fate of the two islands to the north and west of the Continent remain in the observer's mind, and he will note, when the shock of what is called "the Reformation" comes, new phenomena attaching to those islands, cognate to their early history.

Those phenomena are the thesis which I have to present in the pages that follow.

What we call "the Reformation" was essentially the reaction of the barbaric, the ill-tutored and the isolated places external to the old and deep-rooted Roman civilization, against the influences of that civilization. The Reformation was not racial. Even if there were such a physical thing as a "Teutonic Race" (and there is nothing of the kind), the Reformation shows no coincidence with that race. The Reformation is simply the turning back of that tide of Roman culture which, for five hundred years, had set steadily forward and had progressively dominated the insufficient by the sufficient, the slower by the quicker, the confused by the clear-headed. It was a sort of protest by the conquered against a moral and intellectual superiority which offended them. The Slavs of Bohemia joined in that sincere protest of the lately and insufficiently civilized, quite as strongly as, and even earlier than, the vague peoples of the Sandy Heaths along the Baltic. The Scandinavian, physically quite different from these tribes of the Baltic Plain, comes into the game. Wretched villages in the mark of Brandenburg, as Slavonic in type as the villages of Bohemia, revolt as naturally against exalted and difficult mystery as do the isolated villages of the Swedish valleys or the isolated rustics of the Cevennes or the Alps. The revolt is confused, instinctive, and therefore enjoying the sincere motive which accompanies such risings, but deprived of unity and of organizing power. There has never been a fixed Protestant creed. The common factor has been, and is, reaction against the traditions of Europe.

Now the point to seize is this:

Inimical as such a revolt was to souls or (to speak upon the mere historical plane) to civilization, bad as it was that the tide of culture should have begun to ebb from the far regions which it had once so beneficently flooded, the Reformation, that is, the reaction against the unity, the discipline, and the clear thought of Europe, would never have counted largely in human affairs had it been confined to the external fringe of the civilized world. That fringe would probably have been reconquered. The inherent force attaching to reality and to the stronger mind should have led to its recovery. The Northern Germanies were, as a fact, reconquered when Richelieu stepped in and saved them from their Southern superiors. But perhaps it would not have been reconquered. Perhaps it would have lapsed quite soon into its original paganism. At any rate European culture would have continued undivided and strong without these outer regions. Unfortunately, a far worse thing happened.

Europe was rent and has remained divided.

The disaster was accomplished through forces I will now describe.

Though the revolt was external to the foundations of Europe, to the ancient provinces of the Empire, yet an external consequence of that revolt arose within the ancient provinces. It may be briefly told. *The wealthy took advantage within the heart of civilization itself of this external revolt against order;* for it is always to the advantage of the wealthy to deny general conceptions of right and wrong, to question a popular philosophy and to weaken the drastic and immediate power of the human will, organized throughout the whole community. It is always in the nature of *great* wealth to be insanely tempted (though it should know from active experience how little wealth can give), to push on to more and more domination over the bodies of men—and it can do so best by attacking fixed social restraints.

The landed squires then, and the great merchants, powerfully supported by the Jewish financial communities in the principal towns, felt that—with the Reformation—their opportunity had come. The largest fortune holders, the nobles, the merchants of the ports and local capitals even in Gaul (that nucleus and stronghold of ordered human life) licked their lips. Everywhere in Northern Italy, in Southern Germany, upon the Rhine, wherever wealth had congested in a few hands, the chance of breaking with the old morals was a powerful appeal to the wealthy; and, therefore, throughout Europe, even in its most ancient seats of civilization, the outer barbarian had allies.

These rich men, whose avarice betrayed Europe from within, had no excuse. *Theirs* was not any dumb instinctive revolt like that of the Outer Germanies, the Outer Slavs, nor the neglected mountain valleys, against order and against clear thought, with all the hard consequences that clear thought brings. *They* were in no way subject to enthusiasm for the vaguer emotions roused by the Gospel or for the more turgid excitements derivable from Scripture and an uncorrected orgy of prophecy. *They* were "on the make." The rich in Montpelier and Nimes, a knot of them in Rome itself, many in Milan, in Lyons, in Paris, enlisted intellectual aid for the revolt, flattered the atheism of the Renaissance, supported the strong inflamed critics of clerical misliving, and even winked solemnly at the lunatic inspirations of obscure men and women filled with "visions." They did all these things as though their object was religious change. But their true object was money.

One group, and one alone, of the European nations was too recently filled with combat against vile non-Christian things to accept any parley with this anti-Christian turmoil. That unit was the Iberian Peninsula. It is worthy of remark, especially on the part of those who realize that the sword fits the hand of the Church and that Catholicism is never more alive than when it is in arms, I say it is worthy of remark by these that Spain and Portugal through the very greatness of an experience still recent when the Reformation broke, lost the chance of combat. There came indeed, from Spain (but from the Basque nation there), that weapon of steel, the Society of Jesus, which St. Ignatius formed, and which, surgical and military, saved the Faith, and therefore Europe. But the Iberian Peninsula rejecting as one whole and with contempt and with abhorrence (and rejecting rightly) any consideration of revolt—even among its rich men— thereby lost its opportunity for combat. It did not enjoy the religious wars which revivified France, and it may be urged that Spain would be the stronger today had it fallen to her task, as it did to the general populace of Gaul, to come to hand-grips with the Reformation at home, to test it, to know it, to dominate it, to bend the muscles upon it, and to reëmerge triumphant from the struggle.

I say, then, that there was present in the field against the Church a powerful ally for the Reformers: and that ally was the body of immoral rich who hoped to profit by a general break in the popular organization of society. The atheism and the wealth, the luxury and the sensuality, the scholarship and aloofness of the Renaissance answered, over the heads of the Catholic populace, the call of barbarism. The Iconoclasts of greed joined hands with the Iconoclasts of blindness and rage and with the Iconoclasts of academic pride.

Nevertheless, even with such allies, barbarism would have failed, the Reformation would today be but an historical episode without fruit, Europe would still be Christendom, had not there been added the decisive factor of all—which was the separation of Britain.

Now how did Britain go, and why was the loss of Britain of such capital importance?

The loss of Britain was of such capital importance because Britain alone of those who departed, was Roman, and therefore capable of endurance and increase. And *why* did Britain fail in that great ordeal? It is a question harder to answer.

The province of Britain was not a very great one in area or in numbers, when the Reformation broke out. It was, indeed, very wealthy for its size, as were the Netherlands, but its mere wealth does not account for the fundamental importance of the loss of Britain to the Faith in the sixteenth century. The real point was that one and only one of the old Roman provinces with their tradition of civilization, letters, persuasive power, multiple soul—one and only one went over to the barbaric enemy and gave that enemy its aid. That one was Britain. And the consequence of its defection was the perpetuation and extension of an increasingly evil division within the structure of the West.

To say that Britain lost hold of tradition in the sixteenth century because Britain is "Teutonic," is to talk nonsense. It is to explain a real problem by inventing unreal words. Britain is not "Teutonic," nor does the word "Teutonic" itself mean anything definite. To say that Britain revolted because the seeds of revolt were stronger in her than in any ancient province of Europe, is to know nothing of history. The seeds of revolt were in her then as they were in every other community; as they must be in every individual who may find any form of discipline a burden which he is tempted, in a moment of disorder, to lay down. But to pretend that England and the lowlands of Scotland, to pretend that the Province of Britain in our general civilization was more ready for the change than the infected portions of Southern Gaul, or the humming towns of Northern Italy, or the intense life of Hainult, or Brabant, is to show great ignorance of the European past.

Well, then, how did Britain break away?

I beg the reader to pay a special attention to the next page or so. I believe it to be of capital value in explaining the general history of Europe, and I know it to be hardly ever told; or—if told at all—told only in fragments.

England went because of three things. First, her Squires had already become too powerful. In other words, the economic power of a small class of wealthy men had grown, on account of peculiar insular conditions, greater than was healthy for the community.

Secondly, England was, more than any other part of Western Europe (save the Batavian March),[26] a series of markets and of ports, a place of very active cosmopolitan influence, in which new opportunities for the corrupt, new messages of the enthusiastic, were frequent.

In the third place, that curious phenomena on which I dwelt in the last chapter, the superstitious attachment of citizens to the civil power, to awe of, and devotion to, the monarch, was exaggerated in England as nowhere else.

Now put these three things together, especially the first and third (for the second was both of minor importance and more superficial), and you will appreciate why England fell.

---

26. I mean Belgium: that frontier of Roman influence upon the lower Rhine which so happily held out for the Faith and just preserved it.

One small, too wealthy class, tainted with the atheism that always creeps into wealth long and securely enjoyed, was beginning to possess too much of English land. It would take far too long to describe here what the process had been. It is true that the absolute monopoly of the soil, the gripping and the strangling of the populace by landlords, is a purely Protestant development. Nothing of that kind had happened or would have been conceived of as possible in pre-Reformation England; but still something like a quarter of the land (or a little less) had *already* before the Reformation got into the full possession of one small class which had also begun to encroach upon the judiciary, in some measure to supplant the populace in local law making, and quite appreciably to supplant the King in central law making.

Let me not be misunderstood; the England of the fifteenth century, the England of the generation just before the Reformation, was not an England of Squires; it was not an England of landlords; it was still an England of Englishmen. The towns were quite free. To this day old boroughs nearly always show a great number of freeholds. The process by which the later English aristocracy (now a plutocracy) had grown up, was but in germ before the Reformation. Nor had that germ sprouted. But for the Reformation it would not have matured. Sooner or later a popular revolt (had the Faith revived) would have killed the growing usurpation of the wealthy. But the germ was there; and the Reformation coming just as it did, both was helped by the rich and helped them.

The slow acquisition of considerable power over the Courts of Law and over the soil of the country by an oligarchy, imperfect though that acquisition was as yet, already presented just after 1500 a predisposing condition to the disease. It may be urged that if the English people had fought the growing power of the Squires more vigorously, the Squires would not have mastered them as they did, during and on account of the religious revolution. Possibly; and the enemies of the English people are quick to suggest that some native sluggishness permitted the gradual weighing down of the social balance in favor of the rich. But no one who can even pretend to know medieval England will say that the English consciously desired or willingly permitted such a state of affairs to grow up. Successful foreign wars, dynastic trouble, a recent and vigorous awakening of national consciousness, which consciousness had centered in the wealthier classes—all these combined to let the evil in without warning, and, on the eve of the Reformation, a rich, avaricious class was already empowered to act in Britain, ready to grasp, as all the avaricious classes were throughout the Western world, at the opportunity to revolt against that Faith which has ever suspected, constrained and reformed the tyranny of wealth.

Now add to this the strange, but at that time very real, worship of government as a fetish. This spirit did not really strengthen government: far from it. A superstition never strengthens its object, nor even makes of the supposed power of that object a reality. But though it did not give real power to the long intention of the prince, it gave to the momentary word of the prince a fantastic power. In such a combination of circumstances—nascent oligarchy, but the prince worshipped—you get, holding the position of prince, Henry VIII, a thorough Tudor, that is, a man weak almost to the point of irresponsibility where his passions were concerned; violent from that fundamental weakness which, in the absence of opposition, ruins things as effectively as any strength.

No executive power in Europe was less in sympathy with the revolt against civilization than was the Tudor family. Upon the contrary, Henry VII, his son, and his two granddaughters if anything exceeded in their passion for the old order of the Western world. But at the least sign of resistance, Mary who burnt, Elizabeth who intrigued, Henry, their father, who pillaged, Henry, their grandfather, who robbed and saved, were one. To these characters slight resistance was a spur; with strong manifold opposition they were quite powerless to deal. Their minds did not grip (for their minds, though acute, were not large), but their passions shot. And one may compare them, when their passions of pride, of lust, of jealousy, of doting, of avarice or of facile power were aroused, to vehement children. Never was there a ruling family less statesmanlike; never one less full of stuff and of creative power.

Henry, urged by an imperious young woman, who had gained control of him, desired a divorce from his wife, Katherine of Aragon, grown old for him. The Papal Court temporized with him and opposed him. He was incapable of negotiation and still more incapable of foresight. His energy, which was "of an Arabian sort," blasted through the void, because a void was there: none would then withstand the Prince. Of course, it seemed to him no more than one of these recurrent quarrels with the mundane power of Rome which all Kings (and Saints among them) had engaged in for many hundred years. All real powers thus conflict in all times. But, had he known it (and he did not know it), the moment was fatally inopportune for playing that game. Henry never meant to break permanently with the unity of Christendom. A disruption of that unity was probably inconceivable to him. He meant to "exercise pressure." All his acts from the decisive Proclamation of September 19, 1530, onwards prove it. But the moment was the moment of a breaking point throughout Europe, and he, Henry, blundered into disaster without knowing what the fullness of that moment was. He was devout, especially to the Blessed Sacrament. He kept the Faith for himself, and he tried hard to keep it for others. But having lost unity, he let in what he loathed. Not, so long as he lived, could those doctrines of the Reformers triumph here: but he had compromised with their spirit, and at his death a strong minority— perhaps a tenth of England, more of London—was already hostile to the Creed.

It was the same thing with the suppression of the monasteries. Henry meant no effect on religion by that loot: he, nonetheless, destroyed it. He intended to enrich the Crown: he ruined it. In the matter of their financial endowment, an economic crisis, produced by the unequal growth of economic powers, had made the monastic foundation ripe for re-settlement. Religious orders were here wealthy without reason—poor in spirit and numbers, but rich in land; there impoverished without reason—rich in popularity and spiritual power, but poor in land. The dislocation, which all institutions necessarily suffer on the economic side through the mere efflux of time, inclined every government in Europe to a re-settlement of religious endowment. Everywhere it took place; everywhere it involved dissolution and restoration.

But Henry did not re-settle. He plundered and broke. He used the contemporary idolatry of executive power just as much at Reading or in the Blackfriars of London, where unthinking and immediate popular feeling was with him, as at Glastonbury where it was against him, as in Yorkshire where it was in arms, as in Galway where there was no bearing with it at all. There was no largeness in him nor any comprehension of complexity, and when in this Jacobin, unexampled way, he had simply got rid of that which he should have restored and transformed, of what effect was that vast act of spoliation? It paralyzed the Church. It ultimately brought down the Monarchy.

From a fourth to a third of the economic power over the means of production in England, which had been vested top-heavily in the religious foundations—here, far too rich, there, far too poor—Henry got by one enormous confiscation. Yet he made no permanent addition to the wealth of *the Crown*. On the contrary, he started its decline. *The land passed by an instinctive multiple process—but very rapidly—to the already powerful class which had begun to dominate the villages.* Then when it was too late, the Tudors attempted to stem the tide. But the thing was done. Upon the indifference which is always common to a society long and profoundly Catholic and ignorant of heresy, or, having conquered heresy, ignorant at any rate of struggle for the Faith, two ardent minorities converged: the small minority of confused enthusiasts who really did desire what they believed to be a restoration of "primitive" Christianity: the much larger minority of men now grown almost invincibly powerful in the economic sphere. The Squires, twenty years after Henry's death, had come to possess, through the ruin of religion, *something like half the land of England*.

With the rapidity of a fungus growth the new wealth spread over the desolation of the land. The enriched captured both the

Universities, all the Courts of Justice, most of the public schools. They won their great civil war against the Crown. Within a century after Henry's folly, they had established themselves in the place of what had once been the monarchy and central government of England. The impoverished Crown resisted in vain; they killed one embarrassed King—Charles I, and they set up his son, Charles II, as an insufficiently salaried puppet. Since their victory over the Crown, they and the capitalists, who have sprung from their avarice and their philosophy, and largely from their very loins, have been completely masters of England.

Here the reader may say: "What! this large national movement to be interpreted as the work of such minorities? A few thousand squires and merchants backing a few more thousand enthusiasts, changed utterly the mass of England?" Yes; to interpret it otherwise is to read history backwards. It is to think that England then was what England later became. There is no more fatal fault in the reading of history, nor any illusion to which the human mind is more prone. To read the remote past in the light of the recent past; to think the process of the one towards the other "inevitable"; to regard the whole matter as a slow inexorable process, independent of the human will, still suits the materialist pantheism of our time. There is an inherent tendency in all men to this fallacy of reading themselves into the past, and of thinking their own mood a consummation at once excellent and necessary: and most men who write of these things imagine a vaguely Protestant Tudor England growing consciously Protestant in the England of the Stuarts.

That is not history. It is history to put yourself by a combined effort of reading and of imagination into the shoes of Tuesday, as though you did not know what Wednesday was to be, and then to describe what Tuesday was. England did not lose the Faith in 1550-1620 because she was Protestant then. Rather, she is Protestant now because she then lost the Faith.

Put yourself into the shoes of a sixteenth century Englishman in the midst of the Reformation, and what do you perceive? A society wholly Catholic in tradition, lax and careless in Catholic practice; irritated or enlivened here and there by a few furious preachers, or by a few enthusiastic scholars, at once devoted to and in terror of the civil government; intensely national; in all the roots and traditions of its civilization, Roman; impatient of the disproportion of society, and in particular of economic disproportion in the religious aspect of society, because the religious function, by the very definition of Catholicism, by its very Creed, should be the first to redress tyrannies. Upon that Englishman comes, first, a mania for his King; next, a violent economic revolution, which, in many parts, can be made to seem an approach to justice; finally, a national appeal of the strongest kind against the encroaching power of Spain.

When the work was done, say by 1620, the communication between England and those parts of the ancient West which were still furiously resisting the storm, was cut. No spiritual force could move England after the Armada and its effect, save what might arise spontaneously in the many excited men who still believed (they continued to believe it for fifty years) that the whole Church of Christ had gone wrong for centuries; that its original could be restored and that personal revelations were granted them for their guidance.

These visionaries were the Reformers; to these, souls still athirst for spiritual guidance turned. They were a minority even at the end of the sixteenth century, the last years of Elizabeth, but they were a minority full of initiative and of action. With the turn of the century (1600-1620) the last men who could remember Catholic training were very old or dead. The new generation could turn to nothing but the new spirit. For authority it could find nothing definite but a printed book: a translation of the Hebrew Scriptures. For teachers, nothing but this minority, the Reformers. That minority, though remaining a minority, leavened and at last controlled the whole nation: by the first third of the seventeenth century Britain was utterly cut off from the unity of Christendom, and its new character was sealed. The Catholic Faith was dead.

The governing class remained largely indifferent (as it still is) to religion, yet it remained highly cultured. The populace drifted here, into complete indifference, there, into orgiastic forms of worship. The middle class went over in a solid body to the enemy. The barbarism of the outer Germanies permeated it and transformed it. The closer reasoned, far more perverted and harder French heresy of Calvin partly deflected the current—and a whole new society was formed and launched. That was the English Reformation.

Its effect upon Europe was stupendous; for, though England was cut off, England was still England. You could not destroy in a Roman province the great traditions of municipality and letters. It was as though a phalanx of trained troops had crossed the frontier in some border war and turned against their former comrades. England lent, and has from that day continuously lent, the strength of a great civilized tradition to forces whose original initiative was directed against European civilization and its tradition. The loss of Britain was the one great wound in the body of the Western world. It is not yet healed.

Yet all this while that other island of the group to the North-west of Europe, that island which had never been conquered by armed civilization as were the Outer Germanies, but had spontaneously accepted the Faith, presented a contrasting exception. Against the loss of Britain, which had been a Roman province, the Faith, when the smoke of battle cleared off, could discover the astonishing loyalty of Ireland. And over against this exceptional province—Britain—now lost to the Faith, lay an equally exceptional and unique outer part which had never been a Roman province, yet which now remained true to the tradition of Roman men; it balanced the map like a counterweight. The efforts to destroy the Faith in Ireland have exceeded in violence, persistence, and cruelty any persecution in any part or time of the world. They have failed. As I cannot explain why they have failed, so I shall not attempt to explain how and why the Faith in Ireland was saved when the Faith in Britain went under. I do not believe it capable of an historic explanation. It seems to me a phenomenon essentially miraculous in character, not *generally* attached (as are all historical phenomena) to the general and divine purpose that governs our large political events, but *directly* and *specially* attached. It is of great significance; how great, men will be able to see many years hence when another definite battle is joined between the forces of the Church and her opponents. For the Irish race alone of all Europe has maintained a perfect integrity and has kept serene, without internal reactions and without their consequent disturbances, the soul of Europe which is the Catholic Church.

I have now nothing left to set down but the conclusion of this disaster: its spiritual result—an isolation of the soul; its political result—a consequence of the spiritual—the prodigious release of energy, the consequent advance of special knowledge, the domination of the few under a competition left unrestrained, the subjection of the many, the ruin of happiness, the final threat of chaos.

10

CONCLUSION

The grand effect of the Reformation was the isolation of the soul.

This was its fruit: from this all its consequences proceed: not only those clearly noxious, which have put in jeopardy the whole of our traditions and all our happiness, but those apparently advantageous, especially in material things.

The process cannot be seen at work if we take a particular date—especially too early a date—and call it the moment of the catastrophe. There was a long interval of confusion and doubt, in which it was not certain whether the catastrophe would be final or no, in which its final form remained undetermined, and only upon the conclusion of which could modern Europe with its new divisions, and its new fates, be perceived clearly. The breach with authority began in the very first years of the sixteenth century. It is not till the middle of the seventeenth century at least, and even somewhat later, that the new era begins.

For more than a hundred years the conception of the struggle as an ecumenical struggle, as something affecting the whole body of Europe, continued. The general upheaval, the revolt, which first shook the West in the early years of the sixteenth century—to take a particular year, the year 1517—concerned all our civilization, was everywhere debated, produced an universal reaction met by as universal a resistance, for three generations of men. No young man who saw the first outbreak of the storm could imagine it even in old age as a disruption of Europe. No such man lived to see it more than halfway through.

It was not till a corresponding date in the succeeding

century—or rather later—not till Elizabeth of England and Henry IV of France were dead (and all the protagonists, the Reformers on the one side, Loyola, Neri, on the other, long dead), not till the career of Richelieu in the one country and the beginnings of an aristocratic Parliament in England were apparent, that the Reformation could clearly be seen to have separated certain districts of our civilization from the general traditions of the whole, and to have produced, in special regions and sections of society, the peculiar Protestant type which was to mark the future.

The work of the Reformation was accomplished, one may say, a little after the outbreak of the Thirty Years' War. England in particular was definitely Protestant by the decade 1620-1630—hardly earlier. The French Huguenot body, though still confused with political effort, had come to have a separate and real existence at about the same time. The Oligarchy of Dutch merchants had similarly cut off their part of the Low Countries from imperial rule, and virtually established their independence. The North German Principalities and sundry smaller states of the mountains (notably Geneva) had definitely received the new stamp. As definitely France, Bohemia, the Danube, Poland and Italy and all the South were saved.

Though an armed struggle was long to continue, though the North Germans were nearly recaptured by the Imperial Power and only saved by French policy, though we were to have a reflex of it here in the Civil Wars and the destruction of the Crown, and though the last struggle against the Stuarts and the greater general war against Louis XIV were but sequels to the vast affair, yet the great consequence of that affair was fixed before these wars began. The first third of the seventeenth century launches a new epoch. From about that time there go forward upon parallel lines the great spiritual and consequent temporal processes of modern Europe. They have yet to come to judgment, for they are not yet fulfilled: but perhaps their judgment is near.

These processes filling the last three hundred years have been as follows: 1) A rapid extension of physical science, and with it of every other form of acquaintance with demonstrable and measurable things. 2) The rise, chiefly in the new Protestant part of Europe (but spreading thence in part to the Catholic), of what we call today "Capitalism," that is, the possession of the means of production by the few, and their exploitation of the many. 3) The corruption of the principle of authority until it was confused with mere force. 4) The general, though not universal, growth of total wealth with the growth of physical knowledge. 5) The ever-widening effect of skepticism, which, whether masked under traditional forms or no, was from the beginning a spirit of *complete* negation and led at last to the questioning not only of any human institutions, but of the very forms of thought and of the mathematical truths. 6) With all these of course we have had a universal mark—the progressive extension of despair.

Could anyone look back upon these three centuries from some very great distance of time, he would see them as an episode of extraordinary extension in things that should be dissociated: knowledge and wealth, on the one hand, the unhappiness of men upon the other. And he would see that as the process matured, or rather as the corruption deepened, all the marks were pushed to a degree so extreme as to jeopardize at last the very structure of European society. Physical science acquired such power, the oppression of the poor was pushed to such a length, the reasoning spirit in man was permitted to attain such a tottering pitch of insecurity, that a question never yet put to Europe arose at last—whether Europe, not from external foes, but from her own inward lesion may not fail.

Corresponding to that terrible and as yet unanswered question—the culmination of so much evil—necessarily arises this the sole vital formula of our time: *"Europe must return to the Faith, or she will perish."*

I have said that the prime product of the Reformation was the isolation of the soul. That truth contains, in its development, very much more than its mere statement might promise.

The isolation of the soul means a loss of corporate sustenance; of the sane balance produced by general experience, the weight of security, and the general will. The isolation of the soul is the very definition of its unhappiness. But this solvent applied to society does very much more than merely complete and confirm human misery.

In the first place and underlying all, the isolation of the soul releases in a society a furious new accession of *force.* The break-up of any stable system in physics, as in society, makes actual a prodigious reserve of potential energy. It transforms the power that was keeping things together with a power driving separably each component part: the effect of an explosion. That is why the Reformation launched the whole series of material advance, but launched it chaotically and on divergent lines which would only end in disaster. But the thing had many other results.

Thus, we next notice that the new isolation of the soul compelled the isolated soul to strong vagaries. The soul will not remain in the void. If you blind it, it will grope. If it cannot grasp what it appreciates by every sense, it will grasp what it appreciates by only one.

On this account, in the dissolution of the corporate sense and of corporate religion you had successive idols set up, worthy and unworthy, none of them permanent. The highest and the most permanent was a reaction towards corporate life in the shape of a worship of nationality—patriotism.

You had at one end of the scale an extraordinary new *tabus,* the erection in one place of a sort of maniac god, bloodthirsty, an object of terror. In another (or the same) a curious new ritual observance of nothingness upon every seventh day. In another an irrational attachment to a particular printed book. In another successive conceptions: first, that the human reason was sufficient for the whole foundations of human life—that there were no mysteries: next, the opposite extravagance that the human reason had no authority even in its own sphere. And these two, though contradictory, had one root. The rationalism of the eighteenth century carried on through the materialism of the nineteenth, the irrational doubts of Kant (which included much emotional rubbish) carried on to the sheer chaos of the later metaphysicians, with their denial of contradictions, and even of being. Both sprang from this necessity of the unsupported soul to make itself some system from within: as the unsupported soul, in an evil dream, now stifles in strict confinement and is next dissolved in some fearful emptiness.

All this, the first interior effect of the Reformation—strong in proportion to the strength of the reforming movement, powerful in the regions or sects which had broken away, far less powerful in those which had maintained the Faith—would seem to have run its full course, and to have settled at last into universal negation and a universal challenge proffered to every institution and every postulate. But since humanity cannot repose in such a stage of anarchy, we may well believe that there is coming, or has already begun, yet another stage, in which the lack of corporate support for the soul will breed attempted strange religions: witchcrafts and necromancies.

It may be so. It may be that the great debate will come up for final settlement before such novel diseases spread far. At any rate, for the moment we are clearly in a stage of complete negation. But it is to be repeated that this breaking up of the foundations differs in degree with varying societies, that still in a great mass of Europe, numerically the half perhaps, the necessary anchors of sanity still hold: and that half is the half where directly by the practice of the Faith, or indirectly through a hold upon some part of its tradition, the Catholic Church exercises an admitted or distant authority over the minds of men.

The next process we note is—by what some may think a paradox—also due to the isolation of the soul. It is the process of increasing knowledge. Men acting in a fashion highly corporate will not so readily question, nor therefore so readily examine, as will men acting alone. Men whose major results are taken upon an accepted philosophy, will not be driven by such a need of inquiry as those who have abandoned that guide. In the moment, more than a thousand years ago, when the last of the evangelizing floodtide was still running strongly, a very great man wrote of the physical sciences: "Upon such toys I wasted my youth." And another wrote, speaking of divine knowledge: "All the rest is smoke."

But in the absences of faith, demonstrable things are the sole consolation.

There are three forms in which the human mind can hold the truth: The form of Science, which means that we accept a thing through demonstration, and therefore cannot admit the possibility of its opposite. The form of Opinion, which means that we accept a thing through probability, that is through a partial, but not complete, demonstration, and therefore we do not deny the possibility of the opposite. The form of Faith, where we accept the thing without demonstration and yet deny the possibility of its opposite, as for instance, the faith of all men, not mad, in the existence of the universe about them, and of other human minds.*

When acknowledged and defined Faith departs, it is clear that of the remaining two rivals, Opinion has no ground against Science. That which can be demonstrated holds all the field. Indeed, it is the mark of modern insufficiency that it can conceive of no other form of certitude save certitude through demonstration, and therefore does not, as a rule, appreciate even its own unproved first principles.

Well, this function of the isolated soul, inquiry and the necessity for demonstration for individual conviction through measurement and physical fixed knowledge, has occupied, as we all know, the three modern centuries. We all are equally familiar with its prodigious results. Not one of them has, as yet, added to human happiness: not one but has been increasingly misused to the misery of man. There is in the tragedy something comic also, which is the perpetual puzzlement of these the very authors of discovery, to find that, somehow or other, discovery alone does not create joy, and that, somehow or other, a great knowledge can be used ill, as anything else can be used ill. Also in their bewilderment, many turn to a yet further extension of physical science as promising, in some illogical way, relief.

---

*More precisely, the truth of these propositions is seen intellectually by means of a non-discursive act of the mind, an intuition, rather than by means of faith.—Editor, 1992.

A progression in physical science and in the use of instruments is so natural to man (so long as civic order is preserved) that it would, indeed, have taken place, not so rapidly, but as surely, had the unity of Europe been preserved. But the destruction of that unity totally accelerated the pace and as totally threw the movement off its rails.

The Renaissance, a noble and vividly European thing, was much older than the Reformation, which was its perversion and corruption. The doors upon modern knowledge had been opened before the soul, which was to enter them, had been cut off from its fellows. We owe the miscarriage of all our great endeavor in this field, not to that spring of endeavor, but to its deflection. It is a blasphemy to deny the value of advancing knowledge, and at once a cowardice and a folly to fear it for its supposed consequences. Its consequences are only evil through an evil use, that is, through an evil philosophy.

In connection with this release of powerful inquiry through the isolation of the soul, you have an apparently contradictory, and certainly supplementary effect: the setting up of unfounded external authority. It is a curious development, one very little recognized, but one which a fixed observance of the modern world will immediately reveal; and those who come to see it are invariably astonished at the magnitude of its action. Men— under the very influence of skepticism—have come to accept almost any printed matter, almost any repeated name, as an authority infallible and to be admitted without question. They have come to regard the denial of such authority as a sort of insanity, or rather they have, in most practical affairs, come to be divided into two groups: a small number of men who know the truth, say, upon a political matter or some financial arrangement, or some unsolved problem; and a vast majority which accepts without question an always incomplete, a usually quite false, statement of the thing because it has been repeated in the daily press and vulgarized in a hundred books.

This singular and fantastic result of the long divorce between the non-Catholic mind and reason has a profound effect upon the modern world. Indeed, the great battle about to be engaged between chaos and order will turn largely upon this form of suggestion, this acceptation of an unfounded and irrational authority.

Lastly, there is of the major consequences of the Reformation that phenomenon which we have come to call "Capitalism," and which many, recognizing its universal evil, wrongly regard as the prime obstacle to right settlement of human society and to the solution of our now intolerable modern strains.

What is called "Capitalism" arose directly in all its branches from the isolation of the soul. That isolation permitted an unrestricted competition. It gave to superior cunning and even to superior talent an unchecked career. It gave every license to greed. And on the other side it broke down the corporate bonds whereby men maintain themselves in an economic stability. Through it there arose in England first, later throughout the more active Protestant nations, and later still in various degrees throughout the rest of Christendom, a system under which a few possessed the land and the machinery of production, and the many were gradually dispossessed. The many thus dispossessed could only exist upon doles meted out by the possessors, nor was human life a care to these. The possessors also mastered the state and all its organs—hence the great National Debts which accompanied the system: hence even the financial hold of distant and alien men upon subject provinces of economic effort: hence the draining of wealth not only from increasingly dissatisfied subjects overseas, but from the individual producers of foreign independent states.

The true conception of property disappears under such an arrangement, and you naturally get a demand for relief through the denial of the principle of ownership altogether. Here again, as in the matter of the irrational *tabus* and of skepticism, two apparently contradictory things have one root: Capitalism, and the ideal inhuman system (not realizable) called Socialism—both spring from one type of mind and both apply to one kind of diseased society.

Against both, the pillar of reaction is peasant society, and peasant society has proved throughout Europe largely coördinate with the remaining authority of the Catholic Church. For a peasant society does not mean a society composed of peasants, but one in which modern Industrial Capitalism yields to agriculture, and in which agriculture is, in the main, conducted by men possessed in part or altogether of their instruments of production and of the soil, either through ownership or customary tenure. In such a society all the institutions of the state repose upon an underlying conception of secure and well-divided private property which can never be questioned and which colors all men's minds. And that doctrine, like every other sane doctrine, though applicable only to temporal conditions, has the firm support of the Catholic Church.

So things have gone. We have reached at last, as the final result of that catastrophe three hundred years ago, a state of society which cannot endure and a dissolution of standards, a melting of the spiritual framework, such that the body politic fails. Men everywhere feel that an attempt to continue down this endless and ever-darkening road is like the piling up of debt. We go further and further from a settlement. Our various forms of knowledge diverge more and more. Authority, the very principle of life, loses its meaning, and this awful edifice of civilization which we have inherited, and which is still our trust, trembles and threatens to crash down. It is clearly insecure. It may fall in any moment. We who still live may see the ruin. But ruin when it comes is not only a sudden, it is also a final, thing.

In such a crux there remains the historical truth: that this our European structure, built upon the noble foundations of classical antiquity, was formed through, exists by, is consonant to, and will stand only in the mold of, the Catholic Church.

Europe will return to the Faith, or she will perish.

The Faith is Europe. And Europe is the Faith.

NOTES

NOTES

If you have enjoyed this book, consider making your next selection from among the following . . .

Prices subject to change.

Visits to the Blessed Sacrament. *St. Alphonsus* 5.00
Moments Divine—Before the Blessed Sacrament. *Reuter* 10.00
Miraculous Images of Our Lady. *Cruz* 21.50
Miraculous Images of Our Lord. *Cruz* 16.50
Raised from the Dead. *Fr. Hebert* 18.50
Love and Service of God, Infinite Love. *Mother Louise Margaret* 15.00
Life and Work of Mother Louise Margaret. *Fr. O'Connell* 15.00
Autobiography of St. Margaret Mary 7.50
Thoughts and Sayings of St. Margaret Mary 6.00
The Voice of the Saints. *Comp. by Francis Johnston* 8.00
The 12 Steps to Holiness and Salvation. *St. Alphonsus* 9.00
The Rosary and the Crisis of Faith. *Cirrincione & Nelson* 2.00
Sin and Its Consequences. *Cardinal Manning* 9.00
St. Francis of Paola. *Simi & Segreti* 9.00
Dialogue of St. Catherine of Siena. *Transl. Algar Thorold* 12.50
Catholic Answer to Jehovah's Witnesses. *D'Angelo* 13.50
Twelve Promises of the Sacred Heart. (100 cards) 5.00
Life of St. Aloysius Gonzaga. *Fr. Meschler* 13.00
The Love of Mary. *D. Roberto* 9.00
Begone Satan. *Fr. Vogl* 4.00
The Prophets and Our Times. *Fr. R. G. Culleton* 15.00
St. Therese, The Little Flower. *John Beevers* 7.50
St. Joseph of Copertino. *Fr. Angelo Pastrovicchi* 8.00
Mary, The Second Eve. *Cardinal Newman* 4.00
Devotion to Infant Jesus of Prague. *Booklet* 1.50
Reign of Christ the King in Public & Private Life. *Davies* 2.00
The Wonder of Guadalupe. *Francis Johnston* 9.00
Apologetics. *Msgr. Paul Glenn* 12.50
Baltimore Catechism No. 1 .... 5.00
Baltimore Catechism No. 2 .... 7.00
Baltimore Catechism No. 3 .... 11.00
An Explanation of the Baltimore Catechism. *Fr. Kinkead* 18.00
Bethlehem. *Fr. Faber* 20.00
Bible History. *Schuster* 16.50
Blessed Eucharist. *Fr. Mueller* 10.00
Catholic Catechism. *Fr. Faerber* 9.00
The Devil. *Fr. Delaporte* 8.50
Dogmatic Theology for the Laity. *Fr. Premm* 21.50
Evidence of Satan in the Modern World. *Cristiani* 14.00
Fifteen Promises of Mary. (100 cards) 5.00
Life of Anne Catherine Emmerich. 2 vols. *Schmoeger* 48.00
Life of the Blessed Virgin Mary. *Emmerich* 18.00
Manual of Practical Devotion to St. Joseph. *Patrignani* 17.50
Prayer to St. Michael. (100 leaflets) 5.00
Prayerbook of Favorite Litanies. *Fr. Hebert* 12.50
Preparation for Death. (Abridged). *St. Alphonsus* 12.00
Purgatory Explained. *Schouppe* 16.50
Purgatory Explained. (pocket, unabr.). *Schouppe* 12.00
Fundamentals of Catholic Dogma. *Ludwig Ott* 27.50
Spiritual Conferences. *Faber* 18.00
Trustful Surrender to Divine Providence. *Bl. Claude* 7.00
Wife, Mother and Mystic. *Bessieres* 10.00
The Agony of Jesus. *Padre Pio* 3.00

Prices subject to change.

Prices subject to change.

St. Vincent Ferrer. *Fr. Pradel, O.P.* 9.00
The Life of Father De Smet. *Fr. Laveille, S.J.* 18.00
Glories of Divine Grace. *Fr. Matthias Scheeben* 18.00
Holy Eucharist—Our All. *Fr. Lukas Etlin* 3.00
Hail Holy Queen (from *Glories of Mary*). *St. Alphonsus* 9.00
Novena of Holy Communions. *Lovasik* 2.50
Brief Catechism for Adults. *Cogan.* 12.50
The Cath. Religion—Illus./Expl. for Child, Adult, Convert. *Burbach* 12.50
Eucharistic Miracles. *Joan Carroll Cruz.* 16.50
The Incorruptibles. *Joan Carroll Cruz* 16.50
Secular Saints: 250 Lay Men, Women & Children. PB. *Cruz.* 35.00
Pope St. Pius X. *F. A. Forbes* 11.00
St. Alphonsus Liguori. *Frs. Miller and Aubin* 18.00
Self-Abandonment to Divine Providence. *Fr. de Caussade, S.J.* 22.50
The Song of Songs—A Mystical Exposition. *Fr. Arintero, O.P.* 21.50
Prophecy for Today. *Edward Connor* 7.50
Saint Michael and the Angels. *Approved Sources* 9.00
Dolorous Passion of Our Lord. *Anne C. Emmerich.* 18.00
Modern Saints—Their Lives & Faces, Book I. *Ann Ball.* 21.00
Modern Saints—Their Lives & Faces, Book II. *Ann Ball.* 23.00
Our Lady of Fatima's Peace Plan from Heaven. *Booklet.* 1.00
Divine Favors Granted to St. Joseph. *Père Binet.* 7.50
St. Joseph Cafasso—Priest of the Gallows. *St. John Bosco.* 6.00
Catechism of the Council of Trent. *McHugh/Callan.* 27.50
The Foot of the Cross. *Fr. Faber.* 18.00
The Rosary in Action. *John Johnson* 12.00
Padre Pio—The Stigmatist. *Fr. Charles Carty* 16.50
Why Squander Illness? *Frs. Rumble & Carty* 4.00
The Sacred Heart and the Priesthood. *de la Touche* 10.00
Fatima—The Great Sign. *Francis Johnston* 12.00
Heliotropium—Conformity of Human Will to Divine. *Drexelius* 15.00
Charity for the Suffering Souls. *Fr. John Nageleisen* 18.00
Devotion to the Sacred Heart of Jesus. *Verheylezoon* 16.50
Who Is Padre Pio? *Radio Replies Press* 3.00
The Stigmata and Modern Science. *Fr. Charles Carty* 2.50
St. Anthony—The Wonder Worker of Padua. *Stoddard.* 7.00
The Precious Blood. *Fr. Faber* 16.50
The Holy Shroud & Four Visions. *Fr. O'Connell* 3.50
Clean Love in Courtship. *Fr. Lawrence Lovasik* 4.50
The Secret of the Rosary. *St. Louis De Montfort.* 5.00
The History of Antichrist. *Rev. P. Huchede.* 4.00
St. Catherine of Siena. *Alice Curtayne* 16.50
Where We Got the Bible. *Fr. Henry Graham* 8.00
Hidden Treasure—Holy Mass. *St. Leonard.* 7.50
Imitation of the Sacred Heart of Jesus. *Fr. Arnoudt* 18.50
The Life & Glories of St. Joseph. *Edward Thompson.* 16.50
Père Lamy. *Biver.* 15.00
Humility of Heart. *Fr. Cajetan da Bergamo* 9.00
The Curé D'Ars. *Abbé Francis Trochu.* 24.00
Love, Peace and Joy. (St. Gertrude). *Prévot* 8.00

At your Bookdealer or direct from the Publisher.
Toll-Free 1-800-437-5876   *Fax 815-226-7770*

Prices subject to change.

ABOUT THE AUTHOR

Hilaire Belloc
1870-1953

The great Hilaire Belloc was likely the most famous and influential Catholic historian of the past two centuries. His rare understanding of the central role of the Catholic Faith in forming Western Civilization—from the time of Christ up to our own—still opens the eyes of many today.

Hilaire Belloc was born in 1870 at La Celle, St. Cloud, France. His father was a distinguished French lawyer; his mother was English. After his father's death, the family moved to England. Hilaire did his military service in France, then returned to Balliol College, Oxford, taking first-class honors in history when he graduated in 1895. It has been said that his ambition was to rewrite the Catholic history of his two fatherlands, France and England. In 1896 he married Elodie Hogan of Napa, California; the marriage was blessed with two sons and two daughters.

During a period of 50 years—until he suffered a stroke in 1946—Hilaire Belloc wrote over a hundred books on history, economics, military science and travel, plus novels and poetry. He also wrote hundreds of magazine and newspaper articles. He served for a time as a member of the English House of Commons and edited a paper called the *Eye-Witness*.

As an historian, Belloc is largely responsible for correcting the once nearly universal *Whig* interpretation of British history, which attributed Britain's greatness to her Anglo-Saxon and Protestant background.

Hilaire Belloc visited the United States several times, giving guest lectures at both Notre Dame and Fordham Universities. Among his most famous books are *The Great Heresies, Survivals and New Arrivals* (something of a sequel to the above), *The Path to Rome, Characters of the Reformation,* and *How the Reformation Happened.* Hilaire Belloc died in 1953, leaving behind a great legacy of insight regarding the true, though largely unrecognized, inspirer of Western Civilization—the Catholic Church.